Economic Effects of S
on Southern Afri

Other titles published by Gower for the Trade Policy Research Centre

Gary Banks and Jan Tumlir, *Economic Policy and the Adjustment Problem*

Richard Pryke, *Competition among Interternational Airlines*

The cartoon by Berry which appears on the cover was published in *The Star*, Johannesburg, on 8 October 1986.

Thames Essay No. 53

Economic Effects
of Sanctions
on Southern Africa

BY

J.P. Hayes

Gower

Aldershot · Brookfield USA · Hong Kong · Singapore · Sydney

for the

TRADE POLICY RESEARCH CENTRE
London

First published 1987 by

Gower Publishing Company Limited, Gower House, Croft Road, Aldershot,
Hampshire GU11 3HR, United Kingdom

Gower Publishing Company, Old Post Road, Brookfield,
Vermont 05036, United States of America

Gower Publishing Australia, 85 Whiting Street, Artamon,
New South Wales 2064, Australia

ISSN 0306-6991
ISBN 0 566 05539 2

British Library Cataloguing-in-Publication Data
Hayes, J.P.
    Economic effects of sanctions on Southern
Africa
    (Thames essay, no. 53)
    1. Economic sanctions —— South Africa
I. Title   II. Trade Policy Research Centre
III. Series
337.68   HF1613·4

Printed in the United Kingdom by
Biddles Ltd, Guildford, Surrey

Contents

List of Tables

Biographical Note

J.P. HAYES, a Senior Fellow at the Trade Policy Research Centre since 1984, was previously Assistant Under-Secretary of State in charge of the economic advisers at the Foreign and Commonwealth Office in the British Government (1975-84). Mr Hayes has had wide experience in international economic organizations. In 1973-75, he was Director of the Trade and Finance Division at the Commonwealth Secretariat, in London. Before then, in 1971-73, he was Director of the Economic Analysis and Projections Department at the World Bank, in Washington, having also worked at the bank in 1958-64 on economic projections and debt-servicing problems. In 1964-67, Mr Hayes was Head of the Economic Development Division at the Organisation for Economic Cooperation and Development (OECD), in Paris.

After graduating in economics from the University of Oxford, Mr Hayes was awarded a research fellowship, enabling him to do a study on industrial development in the Gulf Coast of Texas in the United States. He then joined the research staff of Political and Economic Planning, in London (1950-53), which has since become the Institute of Policy Studies. Later, he went to the Organisation for European Economic Cooperation (1953-58), the predecessor in Paris of the OECD. After serving in the World Bank and the OECD, Mr Hayes returned to London, joining the Ministry of Overseas Development (now the Overseas Development Administration of the Foreign and Commonwealth Office), first as Director of the World Economy Division, then as Deputy Director-General of Economic Planning.

At the Trade Policy Research Centre, Mr Hayes has been working on a book-length study, *The Making of Trade Policy in the European Community*, to be published shortly. He has published a number of articles and contributed to several volumes of essays.

Preface

ECONOMIC measures against South Africa over her policies of *apartheid* increased significantly in 1985 and 1986. Boycotts of South African goods by private parties in foreign markets and divestment and disinvestment by foreign firms and banks in the Republic, not to mention the international compaign against sporting and cultural ties with South Africa, have led to limited trade sanctions being imposed by the governments of the United States, the European Community, Japan and other countries. Pressures for more extensive sanctions continue in the United Nations and elsewhere.

Policies of racial discrimination and repression in South Africa arouse strong feelings in the Republic itself, in neighbouring countries and in many other parts of the world. The historical, communal, social, economic, political and diplomatic issues involved are complex and they are by no means peculiar to South Africa.

These issues are not broached in this Thames Essay. Nor does the essay go into the efficacy of economic sanctions as an instrument of foreign policy, a subject dealt with recently in other studies. The scope of the essay is limited to the economics of sanctions against South Africa, to assessing the effects of sanctions on the country, on its neighbours and on those imposing them. It is only in this respect that the essay aims to make a contribution to public discussion and policy formation.

In carrying out the study, Philip Hayes was seriously handicapped by the paucity of reliable data (especially on transactions between South Africa and neighbouring countries), some figures being non-existent while much official data is not available. Mr Hayes, a Senior Fellow at the Trade Policy Research Centre, has coped with similar situations before in his wide experience in international economic affairs. He was previously Assistant Under-Secretary of State in the British Government's Foreign and Commonwealth Office where he was in charge of the economic advisers (1975-84). Earlier he held senior appointments in the Commonwealth Secretariat in London, at the World Bank in Washington and at the Organisation for Economic Cooperation and Development in Paris.

In preparing the essay, Mr Hayes visited Pretoria and Johannesburg, in South Africa, and Harare, in Zimbabwe, to interview officials and business economists; and, in addition, he received comments on drafts of the paper from officials and business economists in London, Washington and New York. But the views expressed in the essay are entirely Mr Hayes' responsibility.

As usual, it also has to be stressed that the views expressed in the essay do not necessarily represent those of members of the Council or those of the staff and associates of the Trade Policy Research Centre which, having general terms of reference, does not represent a consensus of opinion on any particular issue. The purpose of the Centre is to promote independent analysis and public discussion of international economic policy issues.

HUGH CORBET
Director
Trade Policy Research Centre

London
February 1987

Chapter 1

Economic Sanctions: a Pause for Thought

ON 20 February 1987, a resolution in the Security Council of the United Nations, calling for a broad range of mandatory economic sanctions against the Republic of South Africa, was vetoed by the United States and the United Kingdom. The Federal Republic of Germany also voted against the resolution, while France and Japan abstained. Ten members of the Security Council supported the resolution.

The resolution aimed to make mandatory on all member countries of the United Nations a set of measures similar to those adopted by the United States Congress in October 1986 and voted into force over President Ronald Reagan's veto. The European Community and the Commonwealth have also adopted sanctions packages, although narrower in coverage than that of the United States, while some countries have decreed general embargoes on trade with South Africa. Most capital inflows into South Africa have now ceased, for a mixture of political and commercial reasons, and the withdrawal of foreign-owned firms from operations in the Republic picked up momentum in 1986. The governments of two Southern African countries, Zimbabwe and Zambia, have threatened to take various economic measures against South Africa, but they have been warned against this by aid donors and have taken no action up to February 1987.[1]

Following the debate in the Security Council of the United Nations, there promised to be a pause in diplomatic initiatives, at least until after the general election among white voters in

South Africa in May 1987. It looked as if the election could determine whether the Nationalist Government, which has been continuously in power since 1948:

> would return to the path of reform, prefigured in the speech made by the President, P.W. Botha, on 31 January 1986,[2] leading to the qualified abolition of influx control (the 'pass laws') in June 1986, or
>
> would continue along the path of repression, to which it returned with the announcement of the second state of emergency on 12 June 1986.

Any such pause in the sanctions debate provides an invitation and an opportunity to reflect on the probable effects of the sanctions which have been imposed already and of such escalation as might occur in the future.

ARGUMENTS FOR AND AGAINST

SANCTIONS

The subject of sanctions against South Africa arouses strong emotions. Many feel strongly that they are necessary to bring about political change or, at the least, to give forceful expression to moral disapproval of policies of racial discrimination and repression in South Africa. Governmental sanctions have been linked to demands for specific reforms. For example, the United States legislation expressly provides that the President may lift some or all of the sanctions if the Government of South Africa meets four out of five conditions:

(a) the repeal of the state of emergency;

(b) the release of Nelson Mandela, jailed leader of the banned African National Congress (ANC), and other political prisoners;

(c) the legalization of all political parties;

(d) the holding of negotiations with representative black leaders; and

(e) the repeal of laws regulating where black South Africans may live and work.

Trade officials tend to deplore economic sanctions as being deployed in a morally arbitrary way, aiming at some countries but not at others whose policies might be considered equally reprehensible. They suggest that governments of different political persuasions are likely to choose different targets for the application of sanctions, adding that this is liable to create much uncertainty, all to the detriment of potentially beneficial economic relations.

Other opponents of sanctions against South Africa argue that they will lead to stiffening of resistance to reform, to increased unemployment, to political polarization and violence and to increased hardship and suffering among the non-white population both in the Republic and in the neighbouring countries. But those who argue along these lines risk being branded as supporters of *apartheid* or apologists for business and financial interests. Proponents of sanctions argue that they are supported by black people in South Africa and in the neighbouring countries who have thereby shown that they are prepared to accept any resulting hardship and risk in pursuit of the desired political objectives.

Different views in the outside world on the desirability of sanctions and related measures are reflected within South Africa.

Some in South Africa, as in the rest of the world, hope that sanctions will increase the pressure for reform: 'Why would white South Africans make noises in the United States and all over the world about the disinvestment campaign,' the black labour leader, Cyril Ramaphosa, has asked, 'if they are not worried about it? ... In recent months it has finally resulted in making the government make a number of changes, which people would never [have] thought could be made in this country.'[3]

On the other hand, a leading white opponent of *apartheid*, Helen Suzman, an opposition member of the South African Parliament, has argued: 'The best hope for reform in South Africa lies in the economic advancement of the blacks. Anything that retards the economic advancement of blacks is counter-productive... Blacks are getting the idea that external pressure and non-governability of the townships will give them victory just round the corner. The risk is that Western powers are inadvertently encouraging blacks to launch violence against whites. And then the government is really going to unleash its terrible power on these kids.'[4]

This is the reformist view. Others turn to thoughts of revolution from impatience, from despair or from an identification of *apartheid* with capitalism. With them, the argument that sanctions may militate against reformist progress carries no weight. Brian Dollery, in a study for the South African Institute of International Affairs, has made the point thus:

> 'The liberal or orthodox view holds that the rational economic decision-making of the market system will inevitably erode and destroy the irrational racial prejudice underpinning apartheid. Economic growth, insofar as it hastens the spread of market forces, will assist in the elimination of apartheid... The revisionist or Marxist thesis, in sharp contrast, views capitalism and apartheid as mutually reinforcing systems. Apartheid structures, by creating a "labour repressive" society, facilitate the exploitation of black workers by monopoly capital. In order to secure the continuity of exploitation, capitalists in turn attempt to strengthen, adapt and perpetuate apartheid. Thus any effort which serves to weaken the power of capitalists will contribute to the destruction of apartheid.'[5]

SCOPE OF THE STUDY

This study is concerned with the potential economic effects of sanctions and related measures on South Africa, on the neighbouring countries and on countries, including countries of Southern Africa, which take economic action against South Africa.[6]

Throughout the essay, 'South Africa' refers to the Republic of South Africa, including the quasi-autonomous 'homelands'. 'Southern Africa' denotes South Africa and her neighbouring countries. Included as neighbouring countries are Namibia

(South-west Africa), Botswana, Zambia, Zimbabwe, Malawi, Lesotho, Swaziland and Mozambique. Zambia and Malawi are not adjacent to South Africa, but they are highly dependent on her, not least for access to the sea via South African ports. In this respect, Zaire must also be regarded, to some extent, as a neighbouring country.

The essay considers the effects of measures and actions affecting South Africa which have been taken up to the present and also of further measures which may possibly be taken in the future if political developments in the Republic fail to satisfy governments and public opinion in the remainder of the world. In this connection, 'sanctions' will be used as a generic term to cover actions taken by governments, boycott actions by private parties and divestment or disinvestment by firms or banks (whether the prime motive is political or commercial).

The main emphasis is on economic effects. It is impossible, though, in the nature of the case, to remain wholly and chastely in the realm of positive economics.

In the first place, the effects of sanctions on the South African economy, and on the welfare of different groups in the population there, will depend in some degree at least on government reactions, which may themselves be shaped by political pressures stemming from the effects of sanctions. Many observers expect sanctions to lead to an increase in economic regulations and controls. Some see favourable possibilities, in the promotion of forced-draft import substitution, while others fear that an increase in regulation would exacerbate the adverse effects of sanctions on economic development and welfare. Still others hope that the political impact of sanctions will reinforce the existing arguments in favour of more labour-intensive development, to the benefit of the economy as a whole and of the black population in particular.

Secondly, the political repercussions of sanctions will be scrutinized by the rest of the world and hence will affect the prospects for rollback, or alternatively of escalation, of sanctions. Sanctions may have the desired effect of stimulating beneficial political change in South Africa or, alternatively, they may strengthen the Government's intransigence in the face of external pressures, leading to the maintenance or further escalation of sanctions.

Thirdly, the effects of sanctions on South Africa's neighbouring countries will depend to a considerable extent on the actions taken by these countries themselves and, still more, on South Africa's reactions to hostile measures by her neighbours. In all these ways, the political and the economic dynamics of sanctions interact.

GENERAL ARGUMENTS ON THE EFFECTIVENESS OF SANCTIONS

A common argument against economic sanctions is that experience shows that they can be easily evaded; and that, for this and other reasons, they are seldom if ever successful in bringing about the desired political results. Against this, a recent scholarly survey of 99 cases of economic sanctions over the period 1914-83, carried out for the Institute for International Economics in Washington, concluded that success in securing the desired objectives had been achieved in 40 per cent of the cases. Sanctions have been more successful in the pursuit of some purposes, or in some circumstances, than in others.[7] No attempt will be made in this essay to argue by analogy with other cases or with the history of sanctions in general.

An analogy which springs readily to mind is with the impact of sanctions on Rhodesia after the unilateral declaration of independence (UDI) in 1965.[8] But there are obvious differences. For example, Rhodesia, while land-locked, received support from South Africa, her much larger and economically more developed neighbour, while South Africa is surrounded by hostile countries, but has access to the sea through a number of ports along a 1,600 mile coast line. Moreover, South Africa has a considerably larger, more developed and more diversified economy than Rhodesia at the time of UDI.

Every case of sanctions is no doubt unique in certain important respects. There are certainly enough special features about the cases of South Africa and her neighbouring countries to require that the prospects be considered in the light of the particular circumstances.

LAY-OUT OF THE ESSAY

The first question which has to be considered, in Chapter 2, is the probable nature and extent of sanctions against South Africa, imposed both by the outside world and by the neighbouring countries. The obvious starting point is the sanctions and other economic measures already in force. It is necessary to consider the possible further escalation of sanctions in the future. At the extreme, is there any realistic possibility of universally observed, comprehensive sanctions — even, perhaps, implemented by means of a naval blockade?

Chapter 3 examines the likely consequences for the South African economy of sanctions of varying degrees of severity. This is in any case necessary before reviewing pass-through effects on the neighbouring countries. Chapter 4 considers the possible impact of various sanctions scenarios for the neighbouring countries.

Chapter 5 deals with the costs, arising from sanctions, to countries outside Southern Africa and in particular the United Kingdom. The conclusions of the essay as a whole are summarized in Chapter 6.

NOTES AND REFERENCES

1. *The Times*, London, 24 February 1987.
2. See Anthony Sampson, *Black and Gold: Tycoons, Revolutionaries and Apartheid* (London, Sydney, Auckland and Toronto: Hodder & Stoughton, 1987) p. 225-26.
3. Quoted in Sampson, *op. cit.*, p. 169.
4. Quoted in Sampson, *op. cit.*, pp. 168 and 170.
5. Brian Dollery, *Has the Divestment Issue been Carefully Considered?* (Johannesburg: South African Institute of International Affairs,

1986). For a study of the relationship between the economic system and *apartheid*, see Merle Lipton, *Capitalism and Apartheid: South Africa 1910-1984* (Aldershot, Brookfield and Sydney: Gower, 1985).

6. Hedley Bull, the late Montague Burton Professor of International Relations at the University of Oxford, remarked that sanctions may be imposed without any precise idea of the results they might be expected to achieve: 'Frequently, when one country imposes a trade embargo or other form of economic penalty on another, it is not as an alternative to going to war or because economic levers are available that might make it possible to bring an adversary to its knees; it is because something needs to be done to satisfy the expectations of domestic or international public opinion.' See Hedley Bull, 'Economic Sanctions and Foreign Policy', *The World Economy*, London, June 1984, a review article on three books on economic sanctions, including the one cited in the following note.

7. Gary Clyde Hufbauer and Jeffrey J. Schott, assisted by Kimberley Ann Elliott, *Economic Sanctions in Support of Foreign Policy Goals*, Policy Analyses in International Economics No. 6 (Washington: Institute for International Economics, 1983). The conclusions do not lend themselves to a brief summary.

8. See Robin Renwick, *Economic Sanctions*, Harvard Studies in International Affairs No. 45 (Cambridge, Massachusetts: Institute of International Studies, 1981).

Chapter 2

Sanctions, Present
Prospective

THIS CHAPTER reviews the history of economic sanctions against South Africa up to February 1987 and considers the prospects for the future.

Sanctions to Early 1987

The history of sanctions, or calls for sanctions, against South Africa goes back as far as 1962, but the movement picked up momentum in 1985 and 1986.[1]

Resolution 1761 in the General Assembly of the United Nations, passed in November 1962, called on members to break diplomatic relations with South Africa, to close their ports to South African vessels, to forbid vessels under their flags to enter South African ports, to boycott trade with South Africa and to suspend landing rights for South African aircraft. This resolution was of little effect. In 1964, however, the Indian Government imposed a total ban on trade with South Africa, but there are reports of evasion, for example, by shipping goods by indirect routes.

The Organization of African States was established in June 1963. It recommended economic sanctions against South Africa, termination of diplomatic links and denial of over-flying rights.

Resolution 181 in the Security Council of the United Nations, passed in August 1963, called on all states to cease shipments of arms to South Africa. This was supported by the United States, but the United Kingdom and France abstained. In July 1970, Resolution 282 of the Security Council extended the arms embargo.

In November 1973 the Organization of Arab Petroleum Exporting Countries (OAPEC) imposed a total ban on sales of oil to South Africa. Under guidelines adopted in 1979, North Sea oil of the United Kingdom has not been exported to South Africa. The OAPEC ban has caused serious problems in South Africa during the periods when oil supplies have been tight, but at other times South Africa has been able to buy without major difficulty on the spot market.

In March 1977, the Reverend Leon Sullivan, a member of the board of General Motors in the United States, drew up a code of employment practices and campaigned for observance by other American-based enterprises operating in South Africa. The Sullivan Code was further elaborated in July 1978. The European Community also adopted a code in 1977, but the British journalist, Anthony Sampson, states in his recent book on South Africa that this was 'widely disregarded'.[2] The Community's code was amended in November 1985.

In 1977, the Security Council of the United Nations adopted a mandatory embargo on the sale of arms to South Africa. Also in 1977, the Commonwealth Heads of Government subscribed to the Gleneagles Agreement discouraging sporting contacts with South Africa.

From the mid-1960s, banks and other firms in the United States began to face hostile questions about their dealings with South Africa, but the pressure built up sharply in 1985.[3] This 'hassle factor' was reinforced by ebbing confidence in South Africa's economic future. In July 1985 the Chase Manhattan Bank refused to roll over its loans to South Africa and other banks in the United States and elsewhere soon followed. There have been a series of divestment or disinvestment decisions by American and other companies, reaching a climax in October and November 1986 with the announcements by IBM, General Motors and Barclays Bank that they were selling their interests in South Africa. (The economic implications of these developments will be considered in Chapter 3 below.) From November 1985 there has been a general prohibition of loans by American financial institutions to the South African Government, or entities owned or controlled by it, except for loans and credits which would improve the welfare of those disadvantaged by *apartheid*.

In September 1985, the European Community adopted the 'Luxembourg package'. Besides confirming the ban on sales to South Africa of arms and para-military equipment, this banned the sale of sensitive equipment to the South African police, the sale of oil to South Africa and cooperation in nuclear development; and it discouraged participation in scientific or cultural events unless they contributed to the ending of *apartheid* or had no possible role in supporting it. In November 1985, the Prime Minister of France, then Laurent Fabius, ordered the parastatal coal and electricity companies to refrain from renewing contracts for the purchase of South African coal.

In October 1985, the Commonwealth Heads of Government, meeting in Nassau, agreed on:

(a) a ban on all new government loans to the South African Government and its agencies and readiness to take whatever unilateral action might be possible to prohibit imports of Krugerrands;

(b) a ban on the sale and export of oil to South Africa;

(c) a ban on new contracts for the sale and export of nuclear goods, materials and technology;

(d) a ban on the sale and export of computer equipment capable of use by the South African military forces, police or security forces;

(e) an embargo on all military cooperation;

(f) a strict and rigorously controlled embargo on imports of arms, ammunition, military vehicles and para-military equipment from South Africa;

(g) the cessation of government funding for trade missions to South Africa or for participation in exhibitions and trade fairs there; and

(h) the discouragement of all cultural and scientific events except where they contribute towards the ending of *apartheid* or have no possible role in promoting it.

For the United Kingdom, this agreement made little addition to the measures already in force. Other possible measures were to be reconsidered at a review meeting in London in August 1986 after a mission to South Africa by the Commonwealth Group of Eminent Persons.[4] The Group's report was highly critical of the South African Government. A further set of measures was agreed at the review meeting by heads of government from Canada, Australia, India, Zimbabwe, Zambia, the Bahamas and the United Kingdom in August 1986, although the Prime Minister of the United Kingdom, Margaret Thatcher, largely abstained. The measures agreed were

(a) a ban on imports of agricultural products from, and all government procurement in, South Africa,

(b) prohibition of government contracts with majority-owned South African companies,

(c) a ban on all new investment or reinvestment of profits earned in South Africa,

(d) termination of all government assistance to, investment in and trade with South Africa,

(e) termination of double-taxation agreements and

(f) suspension of air links and a ban on promotion of tourism in South Africa.

Also agreed, subject to United Kingdom reservations, were

(g) a prohibition of imports from South Africa of coal, iron and steel and uranium,

(h) a ban on all new bank loans to South Africa, whether to the public or the private sectors, and

(i) the withdrawal of all consular facilities in South Africa, except for own nationals and nationals of third countries to whom consular services are rendered.

Canada, Australia and New Zealand have taken steps to implement all or most of the measures. Mrs Thatcher only agreed to voluntary bans on new investment and on promotion of tourism. But she said that if the rest of the European Community agreed to prohibit imports of South African coal, iron and steel, the British Government would not stand in the way.

The Prime Minister of Zimbabwe, Robert Mugabe, and the President of Zambia, Kenneth Kaunda, have been among the most insistent advocates of sanctions. Following the Commonwealth review meeting, Mr Mugabe undertook to implement the entire Commonwealth package, including suspension of air links, and to block financial remittances to South Africa as well. He then turned his attention, in cooperation with Zambia and Denmark, to the possibilities of promoting a broader sanctions resolution in the Security Council of the United Nations.[5] Up to the end of February 1987, the Government of Zimbabwe had not taken action. President Kaunda has been less specific about the action Zambia might take.

In September 1986, the European Community agreed to prohibit imports of South African iron and steel (but not ferro-alloys). A ban on imports of coal was defeated by the strong resistance of the Federal Republic of Germany, Italy and Portugal. After further consideration, the Community agreed on the prohibition of imports of Krugerrands. It also agreed guidelines on investment in and lending to South Africa, to be implemented on an individual basis by member states. Under the guidelines, there would be a ban on 'establishment and extension of branches or new undertakings belonging solely to the person providing the capital and the acquisition in full of existing undertakings, new or increased participation in new or existing undertakings', and 'long-term loans of a participative nature which are made for the purpose of establishing lasting links'. Under the guidelines, countries would not prohibit direct investments made with a view to maintaining the level of existing operations, investments in training or social welfare projects, portfolio investments or reinvestment of profits. There is a potential loophole through investments by subsidiaries in non-Community countries.

Japan promptly followed the European Community in prohibiting imports of South African iron and steel and also banned imports of ferro-alloys.

In October 1986, the United States Congress overrode the President's veto and imposed the broadest package of sanctions yet adopted by any major economic power. The principal measures were:

(a) a prohibition of imports of South African iron and steel, farm products and arms;

(b) a ban after 90 days on imports of coal, textiles and uranium;

(c) a ban on exports to South Africa of crude oil, petroleum products, nuclear materials and technology and arms; and

(d) a prohibition of exports of computers, software and services to any agency involved in the administration of *apartheid*.

United States agencies were prohibited from buying South African goods and services or promoting trade and tourism. Landing rights for South African Airways in the United States were suspended, thus severing direct air links, since no United States airline was still flying to South Africa. Much has remained to be done, after the passage of the bill, to clarify its practical implications.

This summary leaves out of account the broader trade prohibitions adopted by countries such as Norway and Denmark with less weight in international trade. In November 1986, Hong Kong prohibited imports of South African iron and steel, blocking off an important outlet in Asia.

PROSPECTS FOR SANCTIONS

What are the prospects for a rollback of sanctions in the next few years?

As was mentioned in Chapter 1, the United States legislation specifies that the President may lift some or all of the sanctions if the Government of South Africa meets four out of five stated political conditions. The Commonwealth Nassau agreement of October 1985 is linked to a similar set of conditions.

It appears extremely unlikely that these conditions will be met. It is therefore more likely that sanctions will escalate — with continuing dissatisfaction with political developments in South Africa — than that they will be removed. (Indeed, to the extent that sanctions prolong or exacerbate the depressed state of the South African economy, they may well lead to a deterioration, rather than an improvement, in the political situation. Some whites experiencing or threatened by unemployment may become more intransigent, while still greater unrest among blacks, provoked by further increases in unemployment, would be likely to prolong repressive policing, which would become still more severe.)

The veto by the United States and the United Kingdom of a resolution in the Security Council of the United Nations calling for a broad package of mandatory sanctions was noted in Chapter 1.

There has been speculation in South Africa that a resolution in the Security Council on a 'best endeavours' basis might escape the veto, should the sponsors choose to introduce it.

A second possibility is a further steep increase of sanctions if a Democratic, pro-sanctions President is elected in the United States in 1988 and a Labour Government comes to power in the United Kingdom.[6]

A third possibility is the progressive, gradual reinforcement of sanctions, as it is felt desirable from time to time to show dissatisfaction with developments in South Africa or to renew pressure on the South African Government.

The three possibilities are not mutually exclusive, except to the extent that sanctions might reach a point at which the governments applying them might regard the costs of additional measures as outweighing the benefits.

The question then arises as to the extent to which, and the directions in which, sanctions might be further extended.

It appears very probable that trade sanctions will continue to be directed more to purchases from than to sales to South

Africa. In relation to export sanctions, there is always the argument that, if the home country does not sell, it is simply conceding the market to its competitors. In the case of arms and other equipment for the South African security forces and police, this resistance has been overcome by an aversion to increasing the power of the *apartheid* state (or being seen to do so). But even here, governments are liable to be uneasy that they are surrendering opportunities to suppliers elsewhere and, for example, South Africa has been able to obtain French aircraft from Israel.

The action which would be most damaging to the South African economy would be effective measures to depress the price of gold (as advocated by *The Economist*, of London, in July 1986), since this commodity alone provides nearly half of South Africa's visible export earnings. Strong arguments are advanced that this would be undesirable, infeasible or both. In the first place, experience shows that central banks are unwilling to take action, for example by massive sales of gold to private buyers, which would reduce the value of their own gold holdings. The cooperation of the United States authorities would be essential, but this is thought extremely unlikely. It is pointed out that the external debt of some countries is backed by gold. Deliberate depression of the price of gold would be an affront to the Soviet Union, as a major producer (although this might or might not be deemed desirable in itself). It would harm other gold-producing countries, including Zimbabwe, Ghana and Brazil. As to feasibility, the effectiveness of gold sales in depressing the price would depend on the degree of conviction imparted to speculators that the price would remain depressed. The effects of instituting the policy, and possibly of reversing it subsequently, would be very unpredictable. This essay accepts the conventional wisdom that action to depress the price of gold is infeasible or, even if feasible, is highly unlikely to happen.

Similarly, it is generally thought that action to reduce the profits to South Africa arising from the control over the international diamond market of the Central Selling

Organization (De Beers) can be ruled out as a practical possibility. (It is not clear, in any case, to what extent these profits accrue to South Africa.)

It appears highly improbable that the Western industrialized countries will deliberately deny themselves supplies from South Africa of the so-called strategic minerals (the platinum group, manganese, chromium, vanadium), of which the major alternative supplies come from the Soviet Union or Eastern Europe. South Africa might withhold supplies in an effort to discourage damaging actions by others, or by way of retaliation, or in the hope of increasing earnings by pushing up prices. This would be a dangerous policy, though, encouraging substitution and the development of alternative sources of supply. In Chapter 3, it will be assumed that there will be no action by either side to interfere with trade in 'strategic' minerals. The extent of the danger to importing countries is considered in Chapter 5.

It is clearly no coincidence that the most widely applied sanction is against imports of South African iron and steel, commodities in over-supply in the world, and for which there are strong protectionist pressures in the United States and the European Community. Sanctions against South African textiles and clothing similarly appeal to strong protectionist lobbies in developed countries. Sanctions could readily spread to imports of other South African consumption goods. The case of agricultural products is somewhat more problematical. South African fruits fill a seasonal gap in European markets and there may be some sympathy with the argument that sanctions would impose hardship on a major part of the 'coloured' community (people of mixed race) in the Cape region.

Widespread action has already been taken to block capital flows to South Africa. On confidence grounds, South Africa does not now offer much attraction for lending or investment (except reinvestment of profits which could only be remitted on unfavourable terms through the financial rand mechanism — see Chapter 3). It will be suggested below that, while confidence in the future of the South African economy is reduced by sanctions and the possibility of more to come, a stronger influence is apprehension about future internal political and social developments.

SANCTIONS BY NEIGHBOURING COUNTRIES

Up to the end of February 1987, Zimbabwe had not carried out her threat to introduce sanctions, nor had Zambia. While the intentions of the two governments have been shrouded in secrecy, the delay may suggest second thoughts about the costs of sanction measures and the risks of damaging retaliation by South Africa. (The Commonwealth agreement contains an escape clause, requesting the Commonwealth Secretary-General 'to identify such adjustment as may be necessary in Commonwealth countries affected by [sanctions]'.) In the case of Zimbabwe, several observers consider that failure to carry out the threat to sever air links would be particularly visible so that this, if possibly little else, may be done at some time.

At the other end of the scale, Namibia is administered by South Africa in defiance of the relevant United Nations resolutions. Malawi, under President Hastings Banda, has been less anxious to distance herself from South Africa than the other neighbouring countries. The Government of Mozambique, beset by Renamo guerrillas, is in a very weak position and is highly vulnerable to destabilization by South Africa. The Republic, on its side, derives some value from an additional access to the sea for the north-east of the country by way of the port of Maputo (the capital of Mozambique).[7] It is generally considered that Lesotho and Swaziland are too highly dependent on South Africa to be able to contemplate action (see Chapter 4), although they might make gestures on the tacit understanding that nothing damaging to the Republic, and liable to attract retaliation, would actually be done. In Botswana, President Quett Masire, asked whether he supported the Commonwealth package, replied:

'It may be that various countries can apply the measures in varying degrees. Others may find they cannot, because of their circumstances.'[8]

Informed observers believe that Botswana will not in fact take action. She could be important in providing alternative air links with South Africa if Zimbabwe were to suspend such links.

NOTES AND REFERENCES

1. A potted history of sanctions and of governmental attitudes to them, particularly in the United States, is given in Hufbauer and Schott, *op. cit.*

2. See again Sampson, *op. cit.*, p. 128. In December 1985, however, the British Secretary of State for Foreign and Commonwealth Affairs, Sir Geoffrey Howe, told the Select Committee on Foreign Affairs in the House of Commons, 'We think having more than 90 per cent of over 140 British companies reporting under the Code is a useful pressure'. *South Africa, Minutes of Evidence and Appendices*, Sixth Report of the Select Committee on Foreign Affairs, House of Commons, Session 1985-86 (London: Her Majesty's Stationery Office, 1986), p. 46.

3. Sampson, *op. cit.*

4. Group of Eminent Persons, *Mission to South Africa: the Commonwealth Report* (Harmondsworth, Middlesex: Penguin, 1986). The members of the Group of Eminent Persons were Malcolm Fraser and General Olusegun Obasango (co-chairmen), Lord Barber, Dame Nita Barrow, Sardar Fwaran Singh, Rev. Edward Scott and John Malacela.

5. *The Times*, 24 November 1986.

6. Denis Healey, as the Opposition spokesman on foreign affairs in the British Parliament, has spoken strongly in favour of more comprehensive sanctions in the House of Commons (on 17 June 1986 for example) and before the House of Commons Foreign Affairs Committee (*Minutes of Evidence, op. cit.*, pp. 156-71). While there is pressure in the European Community to agree to a common approach on sanctions, the member governments are unwilling that this should form part of the common commercial policy (policed by the Commission and requiring uniformity), so that there is nothing to prevent some Community countries from adopting tougher sanctions than others (apart from dislike of handing competitive advantages to nationals of other countries).

7. After the death of President Samora Machel, the new

Government of Mozambique renewed the Nkomati Accord, originally signed in March 1984, by which it undertakes not to give support and shelter for guerillas of the African National Congress in exchange for a South African undertaking not to take military action against Mozambique.

8. *Financial Times Survey*, London, 25 September 1986.

Chapter 3

Effect of Sanctions on the South African Economy

THE POSSIBLE effects of sanctions on the South African economy have to be seen against the background of recent developments and the present state of the economy. Even before the imposition of sanctions, the economy was in a far from satisfactory condition.

ECONOMIC BACKGROUND TO SANCTIONS

Underlying the problems of the South African economy is the rapid rate of growth of the population and particularly of the black population in the cities. The total population is growing at 2.3 per cent a year; and the black population, at 2.8 per cent a year. With the continuing influx of blacks into urban areas, the urban black population is growing very much faster still. Over 40 per cent of the black population is under fifteen years of age — a vast cohort of labour waiting to come into the labour market. The total increase in the labour force is of the order of 300,000 a year (including 260,000 blacks). At least 25 per cent of the potential black working population is estimated to be unemployed — around 4 million people.

Various estimates suggest that the gross domestic product (GDP) needs to grow by more than 5 per cent a year in order merely to provide employment for the increase in the labour force. The economy did, indeed, grow at around this rate in the years 1966-71. In the 1970s, however, it was affected by the global recession, with rates of growth from 1972 to 1979 fluctuating widely around an average of about 3 per cent.

There was then a recovery to around 5 per cent in 1980 and 1981. But the fall in the price of gold provoked an actual decline of GDP in 1982 and 1983. The 'mini-boom' of 1984 led to a renewed large deficit on the current account of the balance of payments and a substantial loss of external reserves. The authorities felt obliged to impose severe austerity measures in August 1984 and, as a result, GDP fell back again in 1985. GDP grew at an average rate of only 1 per cent a year in real terms from 1980 to 1985 and gross national product (after deduction of net interest, dividends and other factor income payments abroad) stagnated. The annual increase in wage-earning employment in this period was only 0.6 per cent.

Thus the economy of South Africa was already depressed before the debt crisis of August 1985 (discussed shortly). On the other side of the balance, the American dollar price of gold, which contributes around 45 per cent of South Africa's export earnings, recovered by about 15 per cent from the trough of the first quarter of 1985 to July 1986, with a further upsurge by 25 per cent between July and October 1986 (since when the price has fallen back somewhat). This increase in the price of gold gave a marked boost to the economy in the third quarter of 1986. Given the general state of uncertainty as to both internal and external developments, however, there was only a limited and temporary reversal of the depreciation of the rand, which lost half its value against a basket of the more important currencies between February 1984 and August 1986.

This depreciation of the rand has provided a certain stimulus to South African industries, but gross domestic fixed investment has remained depressed, being 27 per cent lower in real terms in the first three quarters of 1986 (seasonally adjusted) than the average level of 1981-82.

Public expenditure has increased in recent years, in part in an effort to improve housing and education for the black population. At 30 per cent of GDP, it is widely thought to constitute a drag on the economy. A quarter of the active white population, 900,000 in all, is in the civil service (and a considerably higher proportion of the Afrikaner population). Another one third of the white population is employed in the costly and often badly managed public-sector corporations. Direct spending on *apartheid* takes up at least 14 per cent of the budget. For instance, South African taxpayers are now paying more than R1.7 billion for the ten 'homelands'; and the subsidy to bus companies to transport black workers from the townships to their places of work has risen to R130 million. The rate of inflation, as measured by the consumer price index, has been rising since 1984 and is approaching 20 per cent.

TYPES OF SANCTION AND THEIR IMPACT

Of the various external economic actions affecting South Africa up to the beginning of 1987, undoubtedly the most damaging is the group of decisions by governments, banks and firms leading to the virtual cessation of capital inflows. It is arguable that capital inflows would have dried up in any case, even without governmental decisions and the pressures on banks and firms not to deal with South Africa. Investment in the Republic, by both nationals and foreigners, has been discouraged by uncertainties over internal political and social developments — although uncertainty has certainly been increased by sanctions themselves, with the possibility of more to come. Moreover, with the disappearance of OPEC current-account surpluses and with large demands for capital inflows into the United States, as the counterpart of the current-account deficit there, it would have been more difficult in any case for South Africa to attract large amounts of foreign capital.

By comparison, the sanctions affecting South African exports and imports, imposed up to February 1987, are comparatively minor in their effects on the economy as a whole. Leaving aside past problems of oil imports,[1] by far the most important of the present trade sanctions are those on iron and steel. Of the major importers, to date only the United States has banned imports of South African coal. The possibility of more widespread embargoes on South African exports will be considered below.

The following discussion considers first the impact of a continuing cessation of capital inflows. The effects of possible loss of export earnings are then added as a further handicap to the South African economy. As a third layer, this part of the study considers the effects of such matters as denial to South Africa of sophisticated computers, continuing lack of confidence and brain drain exacerbated by sanctions.

RESTRICTIONS ON CAPITAL INFLOWS

An acute financial crisis began with the declaration by the Government of South Africa, on 20 July 1985, of a state of emergency. There was heavy selling on the Johannesburg Stock Exchange and capital flight. A large part of the loans from international banks to South African industries fell due at the end of August. The panic was strengthened by rumours that the Chase Manhattan Bank, Citibank and some other banks would refuse to roll over (replace) these loans. Firms sold rand to buy dollars forward to meet claims for repayment. The rumours were confirmed when Chase Manhattan, followed by a number of other major banks, confirmed that it would not roll over outstanding loans. These actions may have been inspired in part by political pressures, but they also reflected commercial judgments that South Africa had ceased to be a good credit risk.

It was hoped that confidence would be restored by a speech to be made in Durban by President Botha on 15 August of that year. This had been prefigured as announcing a number of reforms, amounting to a 'crossing of the Rubicon'. In the event, the 'Rubicon speech' failed to meet expectations. Early the following morning, the rand fell in Johannesburg by 20 per cent.[2]

In response to this crisis, the authorities imposed on 27 August a standstill on most foreign-debt repayments, effective from 2 September 1985. The standstill did not apply to payments for normal current transactions, including payments of interest and dividends, or to repayments of (i) outstanding amounts due from South African importers to foreign suppliers, (ii) bond issues on foreign stock exchanges and public-sector notes privately placed, (iii) debts to the International Monetary Fund (IMF), (iv) debts guaranteed by foreign governments or their export credit agencies, (v) debt commitments of the South African Reserve Bank and (vi) new loans, not replacing existing loans, granted after 2 September 1985.

Simultaneously with the debt standstill, exchange control on capital transfers by non-residents was re-introduced in the form of the financial rand mechanism. Anyone wanting to transfer capital out of South Africa has to make a deposit in a financial rand account. The foreign-exchange value of the financial rand is determined by the demand by foreigners, who can purchase financial rand for foreign exchange in order to acquire capital assets in South Africa. The mechanism is thus designed to prevent capital flight from imposing a burden on the balance of payments, any outflow over the exchanges having to be balanced by a corresponding inflow. By July 1986, the discount of the financial against the commercial rand had widened to roughly 50 per cent; and it has subsequently widened still further, consequently imposing a substantial penalty on those wishing to transfer capital out of South Africa and providing an incentive to re-invest in the Republic. Authorized debt repayments can be made at the more favourable commercial rand rate.

The banks were highly sensitive about delays in the repayment of the considerable volume of inter-bank loans, which are supposed to be highly liquid assets. They were reluctant, however, to be seen to be negotiating directly with the South African authorities. Accordingly, Fritz Leutwiler, the former President of the Swiss National Bank and Chairman of the Bank for International Settlements, was accepted as an independent arbitrator.

A 'broad consensus of agreement' with the principal foreign creditor banks was announced in February 1986. The South

African authorities undertook to lift the restrictions on repayments of 5 per cent of the standstill debt that had already matured or would mature up to the end of June 1987. Of total external debt in excess of $20 billion, rather over half is covered by the agreed provisions for deferral of repayment. A major review of the debt situation is scheduled for April 1987.

'Implementation of the standstill arrangements and stricter application of the exchange-control regulations ... did not succeed in stemming the outflow of capital from South Africa... The very large increase in short-term capital outflows in the second half of 1985 was accounted for, first, by large repayments on loans that were exempted from the standstill restrictions and that might well have been rolled over if South Africa's credit rating had not been reduced by the imposition of the standstill. Secondly, adverse leads and lags came into operation. For example, switches were effected in the financing of imports from a credit to a cash basis, while some exporters delayed the repatriation of export proceeds by granting credit to their overseas customers for extended periods.

'...At the same time, the steady inflow of long-term capital in the form of net new borrowing by public corporations for all practical purposes dried up completely after the standstill had come into effect.'[3]

Some capital outflows continued in the first half of 1986, although on a reduced scale.[4] Export-credit agencies have continued to provide cover.

With the depreciation of the rand and the depressed state of the economy, South Africa achieved a surplus on current account of nearly R6 billion in 1985. But there was a decline of gold and other foreign reserves attributed to balance-of-payments transactions of R1.3 billion in that year (following a loss of R0.9 billion in 1984). Gross gold and other foreign reserves at the end of 1985 were equivalent to just over three months' merchandise exports.

The prospects for net capital flows are uncertain. The financial rand mechanism prevents net capital outflows as a result of divestment by foreign companies. In the important cases of IBM and General Motors, there have been reports of loans by the parent companies to finance the purchases by the successor South African companies, made in time to beat the deadline in the United States legislation for the prohibition of new loans to South Africa. Capital outflows through such mechanisms as leads and lags in international payments are still possible.

Looking to the future, it appears reasonable to assume that there will be little or no net capital inflow into South Africa while sanctions, political attitudes making for sanctions and acute uncertainties over political and social developments in South Africa persist; and it appears reasonable to assume that there may even be some continuing net capital outflow. It may, indeed, be necessary for South Africa to continue to run surpluses on current account of the order of R5-6 billion a year to cover repayment of external debt.

CONSEQUENCES OF THE DRYING UP OF CAPITAL INFLOWS

What are the likely consequences of cessation of capital inflows for the South African economy (leaving aside, for the time being, the additional adverse affects if sanctions were to cause serious reduction of South Africa's current foreign-exchange earnings)? Can the South African economy sustain any positive economic growth? Is there any prospect that it can avoid further increases in unemployment?[5]

In the short term, there is scope for some increase in economic activity by higher utilization of existing capacity. Experience shows, however, that even increased capacity utilization normally depends on a certain amount of new investment; and, beyond the very short term, further economic growth in South Africa will depend on new investment above that required to keep intact the productive capacity of the existing capital stock.

Total gross savings rates in South Africa have been quite high. It seems reasonably probable that South Africa may be able to continue to generate enough savings to cover external interest and dividend payments, as well as some continuing outflows of capital, while still at least maintaining the productive capacity of the capital stock. Thus, even with continuing capital outflows of the order of R5-6 billion a year (as at 1985 prices), South Africa might still be able to avoid an actual decline in GDP. With zero net capital inflows, South Africa might be able to achieve some positive growth of GDP, although considerably less than the 5 per cent or more which, on the present economic structure, would be needed to avoid a further increase in unemployment. (These propositions are explored in the Appendix.)

POLICY REACTIONS TO THE CESSATION OF CAPITAL INFLOWS

Any such estimates are highly dependent on assumptions about the evolution of the savings rate and the relationship between product growth and capital formation. In principle, future growth prospects could be improved by policies which would increase domestic savings or improve the ratio of product growth to capital formation.

A possibility which is already much discussed in South Africa is a switch to more labour-intensive development, desirable both to economize capital and to reduce unemployment which, if past trends persist, will almost inevitably continue to increase. The common, if not entirely apt, slogan for this approach is 'inward industrialization', which has been defined as the development of industries which meet the needs of newcomers to urban areas, using unsophisticated, labour-intensive methods. Some South Africans see, as mentioned earlier, a possible benefit in sanctions, in strengthening of pressures for a switch to more labour-intensive development.

While the logic is clear, it is less obvious how such a change in the pattern of development could in fact be brought about.

The most usual suggestion is for an effort to promote labour-intensive building of better-located housing for large sections of the black population. This could make a major contribution to welfare. If, however, the programme had to be subsidized to any considerable degree, it could eat into the savings required to build up the other sectors of the economy. (Against this, it is suggested that improved housing, more accessible to places of work, could lead to marked gains in productivity.) A major problem up to the present is the availability of land for black housing. In November 1986, the South African Government, presumably with an eye to elections scheduled for the following spring, refused to consider a major report on the future of the Group Areas Act, the major pillar of the racial zoning of land.

The many onerous restrictions on the operations of black-owned businesses have been progressively removed since the late 1950s, but there remains a mass of regulations and requirements for permits, applied to small enterprises as to medium and large. The South African economy is highly regulated and an army of bureaucrats has a vested interest in the continuation of regulation. Labour-intensive development would require a break with many of the habits of the past. There are many in South Africa, however, who see still more regulation as a necessary and desirable reaction to sanctions. This aspect will be further discussed below in relation to the effects of sanctions restricting South African exports.

Despite the problems, there should be scope for increased sub-contracting of labour-intensive processes.

SANCTIONS AGAINST SOUTH AFRICAN EXPORTS

The probable effect on South African export earnings of sanctions imposed up to the beginning of 1987, while not negligible, is nevertheless fairly small.

Leaving aside import embargoes on Krugerrands, the next most widespread set of sanctions affecting South African exports is on iron and steel. This might affect, say, 3 per cent of export earnings. An estimate from the industry association suggests that some 47,000 jobs could be at risk.

There may well be continuing pressure to increase the range of sanctions against goods exported from South Africa. While it is impossible to predict with any assurance when and what further sanctions might be imposed, it is worth considering the effects of a maximum plausible package of sanctions (falling well short of would-be universal, mandatory sanctions against all South African exports, enforced by a naval blockade).

It has been suggested in Chapter 2 that no action is likely to be taken which would depress South Africa's earnings from gold, diamonds or strategic minerals of which South Africa is a major supplier. (Uranium is not included here as a strategic mineral, which would be untouched by sanctions, since plentiful supplies are available from other sources.) Widespread bans have been imposed on imports of Krugerrands, but the loss to South Africa is only the premium over the value of the gold from which the coins are made, said to be of the order of 3 per cent. This loss is negligible when spread over the total value of gold exports. This suggests that almost 60 per cent of visible exports, by value, are likely to be untouched by sanctions (gold alone amounting to around 45 per cent).

Coal contributes roughly 7 per cent of South Africa's visible export earnings. Up to the end of 1986, while the United States legislation prohibits imports of South African coal, there has been strong resistance in the European Community to similar action. Even if the pressures were to build up for effective sanctions against South Africa by the the Community and Japan, it is commonly considered in South Africa that alternative buyers for coal could be found, in Eastern Europe and elsewhere, although at some discount from present prices. To avoid under-estimation of the possible effect, it will be assumed here that earnings from coal exports might be halved, a loss amounting to about 3.5 per cent of total export earnings.

Roughly 8 per cent of visible export earnings come from

agricultural products, foods, beverages and tobacco, hides and skins and wool. South African fruit (some 1.5 per cent of total visible exports by value), it has been pointed out, fills a seasonal gap in the European market and there is also the argument that sanctions would be a heavy blow to sections of the Cape coloured community. But again, to avoid under-estimation of possible measures, it will be assumed that the whole of this group is at risk.

This leaves about a quarter of visible exports by value, consisting largely of non-strategic minerals and metals (including iron, steel and uranium) and a wide range of manufactured goods. These exports are vulnerable not only to political considerations but also to protectionist pressures. On the other hand, for these and other goods, much thought is already being given to sanctions busting and it is said that individuals, prominent during the period of sanctions against Rhodesia, are again to be seen on the hunt for lucrative pickings. It will be assumed that export earnings from this group might be halved — a loss of about 12 per cent of total visible export earnings — although this might be considered exaggerated, given the possibilities of evasion.

On the basis of these rough and tentative estimates, it would appear that broader sanctions against South African exports might lead to a loss of visible export earnings of almost a quarter, or some R8.5 billion on the basis of 1985 volumes and prices, equivalent to about 7 per cent of GDP.

A study by Edward Osborn, the group chief economist of Nedbank based in Johannesburg, takes a more expansive view of the possibilities of evading sanctions and concludes that 'the impact of total sanctions would be at worst 11.5 per cent of total exports'.[6]

Both estimates depend crucially on the assumption that no effective action will be taken to depress the price of gold and abstract from movements in the gold price which will occur in any case.

As suggested above, it seems unlikely that exports to South Africa will be banned, except for arms and security-related equipment. There is considerable resistance to the proposal to suspend air services to and from the Republic, but this, or suspension by neighbouring countries of over-flying rights, cannot be wholly ruled out.

ECONOMIC EFFECTS OF TRADE SANCTIONS

There are widely differing views on the effects on the economy of sanctions leading to a substantial decrease in South African export earnings:

'There is a fairly widespread belief in South Africa that the application of total sanctions against the South African economy would lead to an initial stimulation of economic growth. While there is general agreement that sanctions would lead to long-term economic decline, the assumption of shorter term growth leads to the prospect of sanctions being viewed by many with a degree of equanimity. This assumption is based, to a large extent, on the Rhodesian experience — a faulty and dangerous comparison because of certain fundamental differences in the two sets of circumstances.'[7]

On the (short-term) complacent view, the stimulus to the economy would come from a boost to import-substitution activities, arising from some combination of depreciation of the exchange rate and additional controls on imports or other protective measures.

South Africa has certain advantages in coping with severe trade sanctions. She is, for example, self-sufficient in food. A large part of total energy requirements is met from indigenous coal. Forty per cent of oil requirements are supplied by the Sasol oil-from-coal plants (although at a fairly high cost). In addition, while information on the subject is a closely-held secret, it is said that South Africa has accumulated large stocks of imported oil — possibly enough to safeguard the energy situation for several years, even against a total cut-off of oil imports.[8] There is a large and comparatively sophisticated manufacturing base.

The fact remains that trade sanctions, coupled with the near cessation of capital inflows, could seriously reduce the capacity to import. South Africa is still quite dependent on imports for machinery and equipment, particularly of a sophisticated nature, and for other productive inputs. About 30 per cent of South Africa's imports by value are machinery, over 10 per cent transport equipment, as much again ores and chemicals; and about 15 per cent is in the unspecified residual group which includes oil as well as military equipment. These categories together make up two-thirds of imports by value.

The Osborn study concludes that imports could be cut by up to 45 per cent without serious impairment of the economy. This is made up of 21 per cent of items considered as inessential and 24 per cent of items judged to be substitutable by domestic production in the short term. A further 22 per cent of imports is judged to be substitutable in the longer term.[9]

There is some scope for import substitution by making fuller use of existing capacity, but beyond this import substitution will depend on investment. While the depreciation of the exchange rate has given some stimulus to manufacturing, gross fixed investment still remained notably depressed in the first three quarters of 1986. In the longer run, the constraint on investment may be the availability of savings; but the confidence factor is also important. In the words of the South African Foundation: 'There tends to be a concentration on the direct effects of sanctions. The intangible effects on business confidence are perhaps the most important.'[10]

A paper, widely publicized, produced in the Federated Chamber of Industries suggests conclusions strikingly at variance with those of Mr Osborn.[11] The paper considers the impact of trade sanctions of three different degrees of severity. It assumes, throughout, that South Africa will not renege on her external debt and will continue to repay 'at a reasonable rate', necessitating continued external surpluses on current account of R5-6 billion a year, as at 1985 prices, or of the same order magnitude as in 1985.

'This approach ... focuses attention on the overall
downward adjustment processes which the domestic
economy as a whole would have to go through in order
to maintain [the assumed surplus on current account].
The basic policy instruments utilised in the adjustment
process are government expenditure, interest rates, the
exchange rate and direct import controls. With the
exception of import control, the adjustment burden was
spread among these instruments in a roughly proportional
manner...

'It was assumed that wherever it could be done imports
would be replaced (or displaced) up to the ceiling provided
by current production capacity. No new investment for
import substitution would, however, be made. In other
words, present unutilised capacity would be filled as far
as possible through a system of direct quantitative
controls.'[12]

The extreme case assumes a reduction of 80 per cent in
most exports except gold, diamonds and certain strategic
minerals. If exports now contributing about 40 per cent of
visible export earnings were cut by 80 per cent, the loss would
be equivalent to 10.1 per cent of GDP, shown as the 'inter-
industry effect' in the paper.[13] The paper then goes on to
estimate that the total net effect over 5 years, after the required
adjustments to maintain the necessary surplus on current
account, would be a decrease in GDP of 29.3 per cent — that
is to say, nearly three times as great as the inter-industry
effect.[14] The corresponding decrease in employment is put at
just over 1 million, equal to almost a quarter of employment
in 1985.

This estimate raises questions on two levels: first, the size
of the export loss assumed to result from sanctions; second,
the extent to which the total net effect, after the necessary
adjustments, is estimated to exceed the loss of exports.

On the first level, it is a rather severe assumption that
exports other than gold, diamonds and strategic minerals would
be reduced by as much as 80 per cent. The rough estimate

of export losses with fairly severe but by no means leak-proof sanctions, set out earlier, suggests that South Africa's export earnings might be cut by almost a quarter, equivalent to about 7 per cent of GDP. This appears to be close to the intermediate scenario in the paper of the Federated Chamber of Industries in which the inter-industry effect is put at a decrease of GDP by 6.7 per cent. The corresponding total net effect is estimated as a decrease in GDP of some 17 per cent (two-and-a-half times as great as the inter-industry effect), with a decrease of employment of just over two-thirds of a million, equal to about 14 per cent of employment in 1985.

A third scenario is based on sanctions as agreed towards the end of 1986. By analogy with the other estimates, it appears that these are assumed to lead to a reduction of export earnings of about 5.6 per cent (1.7 per cent of GDP); and the total net effect might be a reduction of GDP and employment of the order of 4 per cent.

There would appear to be a considerable conflict between Mr Osborn's conclusions and those in the paper of the Federated Chamber of Industries. While there is difficulty in interpreting the figures, the Federated Chamber's paper appears to assume a considerably greater loss of export earnings, even in the intermediate case, than does the Osborn study. Mr Osborn appears to consider that the South African economy could survive severe trade sanctions with comparatively little damage, at any rate in the short run, on the basis of fairly extensive import substitution. By contrast, the Federated Chamber's paper estimates a decrease of GDP of about 17 per cent on the intermediate-sanctions scenario. Clearly, whatever the severity of sanctions, the outcome will be influenced both by government policies (considered further below) and by the reactions of the private sector. The Federated Chamber's paper emphasizes the adjustments needed to sustain large surpluses on current account and it assumes no import substitution beyond what can be achieved by fuller utilization of existing productive capacity. Mr Osborn stresses the possibilities of import substitution. These possibilities, however, would be limited by the availablity of capital and other resources. Capital appears to be plentiful at present, as witness the boom on the Johannesburg Stock Exchange; but this is in considerable part a reflection of widespread reluctance to invest, given the many uncertainties, both internal and external. The estimates in the Appendix suggest that, if it is necessary to run surpluses on current account of the order of R5-6 billion a year to repay external debt in the absence of substantial capital inflows, then the availability of savings might be just about enough to maintain the productive capacity of the capital stock. Investments in particular forms of import substitution would then tend to be at the expense of maintenance of capacity elsewhere in the economy.

Any depression of activity in order to adjust to a reduction in the capacity to import will tend to reduce savings — it is difficult to say by how much. It is possible that even the intermediate case in the Federated Chamber's paper may exaggerate the damage to the economy from fairly severe trade sanctions, but it is difficult to say this with any degree of certainty. The problems of estimation are discussed more fully in the Appendix.

Sanctions may impose other handicaps on the economy besides direct damage to some export activities, limitations in the supply of savings available for the finance of capital formation and contraction of the overall capacity to import. There are fears in South Africa of falling further behind the technological leaders as a result of sanctions and divestment.

It has been suggested above that countries are likely to be unwilling to impose sanctions on their exports to South Africa, except for equipment likely to be used by the security forces and police. Some of the divestment operations — for example those by General Motors and IBM — may not lead to a witholding of technology, at any rate in the short run. Over time, nevertheless, South African firms may have increased difficulty in securing access to the latest technologies.

Furthermore, prolonged or aggravated depression of the economy, and increasing tension and unrest, are likely to

✓ accelerate brain drain further. It is said that this has not yet seriously reduced the productive capacity or adaptability of manufacturing industries. Nevertheless, some professional groups, including accountants, have already been significantly affected. There are fears of disappearance of a 'critical mass' of good people in some institutions of higher education.

EMPLOYMENT EFFECTS

With the drying up of capital inflows, there appears to be little prospect that the South African economy will grow at the rate of over 5 per cent estimated to be necessary to prevent an increase of unemployment, given continuation of the present economic structure. Further depression of economic activity as a result of severe trade sanctions would further exacerbate the unemployment problem. The Federated Chamber's paper estimates percentage reductions of employment at rather less than estimated reductions of GDP. Thus, in the intermediate case discussed above, the reduction of employment over five years is put at 14.2 per cent.

Questions on the potential effect of sanctions on employment were included in a survey of conditions in the labour force carried out by the Bureau of Market Research at the University of South Africa, in Pretoria, in the first half of 1986. A questionnaire was sent to private and public enterprises (but excluding agriculture), central government bodies and provincial administrations.[15] Among a variety of other questions, respondents were asked:

'Have disinvestment and limited trade sanctions, as applied *inter alia* by the USA and EEC countries, had or will they have any effect on your employment figures?

'If 'yes', estimate the percentage change in your employment figures and/or expected change.

'In the event of a total trade boycott against South Africa, would you expect your employment figures to increase, decrease or remain the same?

'If you expect an increase or decrease, please estimate the expected percentage change.'

Unfortunately, the question on the effect of sanctions already imposed was asked before the decisions of the European Community and United States in September-October 1986 and before several of the major divestment actions. Nevertheless, the responses to this question are not entirely without interest. The net decrease of employment was put at 2 per cent. The largest decreases were expected in construction (4.6 per cent), manufacturing (3.8 per cent) and hotels (2.9 per cent). The expected reduction for mining and quarrying was 1.1 per cent. Reductions by racial group were put at 3.6 per cent for coloured (particularly high in manufacturing and construction), 2.2 per cent for blacks, 2.0 per cent for Asians and 1.0 per cent for whites.

The expected decrease in employment as a result of total trade sanctions was put at 13.5 per cent. This result is very close to the decrease of employment equivalent to 14.2 per cent of employment in 1985, estimated on the intermediate scenario in the Federated Chamber's paper. But this finding of the Bureau of Market Research's survey has to be interpreted with great caution, since different respondents would have made different assumptions as to the macro-economic effects on the economy. (The questionnaire, as reproduced in the report, does not indicate that any guidance was given on a framework of assumptions.)

POLICY REACTIONS TO TRADE
SANCTIONS

It has been seen that some in South Africa expect that the initial effect of severe trade sanctions might be a stimulus to the economy through the stimulation of import-substituting activities. This could come about either through further depreciation of the exchange rate (or at any rate persistence of highly competitive rates for the rand as in 1986) or through import controls or other protective measures.

While the Federated Chamber's paper mentions the exchange rate and import controls among the measures assumed to be taken to adjust to contraction of the capacity to import, it is not clear what weight has been given to these policies, as against internal contractionary policies and how their effect has been simulated. The independent simulations reported in the Appendix suggest that the emphasis has been on contractionary policies, with little discernible influence of short-term stimulative influences.

This may well be justified. An immediate effect of either further depreciation of the exchange rate or import controls would be to exacerbate inflation, already approaching 20 per cent a year. This would be likely to have adverse effects on economic development, either directly or indirectly by strengthening the case for contractionary monetary and fiscal policies.

If sanctions substantially reduce the capacity to import, there will be strong pressures, backed by protectionist lobbies and the self-interest of an over-large bureaucracy, to restrict 'inessential' imports. (South Africa is already a highly *dirigiste* economy, so that the tendency to react to economic problems by further controls is already engrained.) Import controls would lumber the South African economy with more high-cost activities and further decrease its ability to take full advantage of the gains available through international trade. Any necessary stimulus to import substitution would be best given through the exchange rate, allowing full play to a price mechanism in touch, so far as sanctions allow, with conditions in international trade.

One evident safety valve, if the capacity to import were really seriously constrained, would be suspension of external debt service and dividend payments. Liabilities on account of interest, dividends, branch profits *et cetera* reached R3,866 million in 1984 (the latest figure available). This figure may be compared with the estimate, above, of a reduction of export earnings by R8.5 billion a year, on a fairly severe sanctions scenario. One usual disadvantage of suspension of external debt-service payments is the drying up of new credit; but, as has been seen above, South Africa has already had to cope with this and has already had to place a substantial part of her imports on a cash instead of a credit basis. There would also be the risk of retaliatory freezing or even expropriation of South Africa's external assets. Earnings from these assets in 1984, however, were R635 million, a fairly small offset to the corresponding liabilities. So far, the South African authorities have been extremely reluctant to suspend interest and dividend payments, seeing political as well as economic disadvantages. (They have wished to present South Africa as an economically well-behaved nation.) But if sanctions were to threaten really serious damage, the authorities might feel themselves obliged to claim *force majeure*. This must be a consideration to governments of creditor countries in deciding how much further to go in imposing sanctions.

NOTES AND REFERENCES

1. President Botha is quoted as saying that by 1983 South Africa sometimes only had enough oil for a week; also that the need to pay premium prices for oil had cost South Africa R22 billion over ten years (speech in Vereeniging, April 1986, cited in Sampson, *op. cit.*, p. 259). More recently, however, South Africa has been able to take advantage of plentiful supplies to rebuild stocks.

2. For a more detailed account and analysis of the crisis, see Laurence Harris, 'South Africa's External Debt Crisis', *Third World Quarterly*, London, July 1986, pp. 793-817.

3. *Annual Economic Report* (Pretoria: South African Reserve Bank, 1986) pp. 20-21.

4. See *Quarterly Bulletin*, South African Reserve Bank, Pretoria, September 1986.

5. For a discussion of the role of foreign capital in South Africa, see Carolyn M. Jenkins, *The Economic Implications of Disinvestment for South Africa* (Johannesburg: South African Institute of International Affairs, 1986).

6. Reported in *Financial Mail*, Johannesburg, 5 December 1986.

7. Memorandum by the South Africa Foundation in *South Africa*, Sixth Report of the House of Commons Select Committee on Foreign Affairs, *op. cit.*, p. 140.

8. But see note 1 above.

9. *Financial Mail*, 5 December 1986.

10. Reference as in note 7.

11. *The Effect of Sanctions on Employment and Production in South Africa: a Quantitative Analysis* (Pretoria: Federated Chamber of Industries, 1986).

12. *Ibid.*

13. This percentage still appears high, on the natural interpretation of the 'inter-industry effect', which might be expected simply to allocate the loss of exports between supplying industries, as is done in the paper. The figure given would not seem to allow for any import content of the lost exports, or for losses of export earnings as a result of price cutting rather than reductions of volume.

14. According to the sort of growth model reasoning set out in the Appendix, capital outflows equivalent to annual surpluses on current account of R5-6 billion might lead to something like stagnation of GDP. The estimated reductions in GDP can probably be treated, therefore, as declines over five years from the level of the base year.

15. P.A. Nel, *An Assessment of the Development and Welfare of Employees in the Republic of South Africa*, Research Report No. 133 (Pretoria: Bureau of Market Research, University of South Africa, 1986).

Chapter 4

Impact of Sanctions on South Africa's Neighbours

DISCUSSION of the potential impact of economic sanctions on South Africa's neighbouring countries is often confused by failure to discriminate between the three aspects of the question:

(a) the pass-through effects of sanctions on South Africa, which would occur even if the neighbouring countries did not themselves apply sanctions against South Africa and the Republic did not take retaliatory or other harmful measures against them;

(b) the cost to neighbouring countries of sanctions they themselves may impose against South Africa; and

(c) the costs to neighbouring countries of possible retaliatory actions by South Africa.

These three aspects will be considered in turn. The chapter ends by considering the prospects for increased aid to compensate neighbouring countries for damage to their economies resulting from sanctions and related actions.

PASS-THROUGH EFFECTS OF SANCTIONS ON SOUTH AFRICA

Even without sanctions imposed by the neighbouring countries and retaliatory action by South Africa, at least several of the neighbouring countries are likely to suffer adverse pass-through effects resulting from sanctions by the rest of the world against South Africa, the more severe the greater the depression of economic activity in South Africa. The impact of sanctions is likely to reduce South Africa's imports of goods and services from her neighbouring countries. Domestic strains may lead South Africa to expel migrant workers, increasing unemployment problems in neighbouring countries, at any rate in the short run, and reducing the flows of worker's remittances.

On the other side of the account, there are certain potential benefits to neighbouring countries resulting from sanctions on South Africa. To the extent that these countries import more goods and services from South Africa than they export to her, they may benefit from the depression of the value of the rand. (There is no such opportunity for Swaziland and Lesotho so long as they remain in the Rand Monetary Area.) Secondly, there may be profits to be made from sanctions-busting activities, for those neighbouring countries which are prepared to encourage or condone them.

South Africa is an important export market for Lesotho (about one-third in 1982), Swaziland (about a quarter in the same year), Malawi (around 20 per cent) and Zimbabwe. (Sixteen per cent or more of Zimbabwe's merchandise exports went to South Africa in 1983 and 1984, although the proportion was down to about 11 per cent in 1985.) On the other hand, less than 1 per cent of Zambia's exports go to South Africa and, it appears, less than 10 per cent of Botswana's. South Africa is a substantial source of tourist revenues for Lesotho, Swaziland, Zimbabwe and Botswana.

It has been suggested above that, if trade sanctions were fairly severe, they might lead to a reduction of South Africa's capacity to import by up to about 30 per cent and, in the absence of major adjustments in the economy, to a substantial reduction of GDP. If there were an equi-proportionate decrease in South Africa's imports from Zimbabwe, for example, this would reduce Zimbabwe's merchandise export earnings by, say, 3 to 5 per cent. This does not appear catastrophic in macro-economic terms, but it would nevertheless increase the already severe foreign-exchange problem (see below). Some manufacturers would be seriously affected. Forty per cent of foreign tourists in Zimbabwe come from South Africa, so that hotel occupancy rates would be further reduced.

About one-third of a million migrant workers from neighbouring countries are legally employed in South Africa, about 80 per cent of them in the mines; and the number of illegal immigrants, many of them working in agriculture, may be very much larger. It has been seen that unemployment is already high in South Africa, particularly among the black population, and it is liable to increase substantially over the coming years. This seems likely to lead to increasing pressures to repatriate workers from neighbouring countries, although there is resistance from employers, who do not want to lose experienced workers. Workers' remittances are of overwhelming importance to Lesotho, where they are said to contribute as much as half of GNP. Remittances as a percentage of GDP are estimated at 6 per cent for Swaziland, 3 per cent for Mozambique, 2 per cent for Malawi and 1 per cent for Botswana.

In the short run, reduction of the number of workers employed in South Africa would exacerbate unemployment problems in the neighbouring countries. The effect in the longer run is more problematical. It is often argued that emigration of labour robs countries of many of the most able-bodied, energetic and enterprising individuals and so imposes a drag on economic development.

ECONOMIC FRAGILITY OF SOME NEIGHBOURING COUNTRIES

As for South Africa, so for the neighbouring countries, the potential effects of sanctions and sanction-related measures have to be seen against the background of the present state of their economies.

Angola and Mozambique are very seriously disrupted by civil war, but are less affected by sanctions and related actions than several of the other neighbouring countries. Mozambique, however, is vulnerable to the effects of repatriation of migrant workers and also to loss of revenue if South Africa were to reduce traffic through the port of Maputo. (Maputo, though, could be important to South Africa as a loophole for the evasion of trade sanctions.)

The economies of Lesotho and Swaziland are highly interdependent with South Africa and the pass-through effects of a severe depression of the South African economy could be considerable. On the other hand, there may be opportunities for substantial benefits from playing host to sanction-busting activities.

In October 1986, South Africa signed an agreement with Lesotho for a major cooperative water development project which, if carried through, will provide substantial benefits for Lesotho as well as for South Africa.

The economy of Malawi has been relatively robust up to the present. But it has suffered from transport problems, notably in exporting sugar. These may be relieved if the Nacala railway line is reopened in the spring of 1987. Malawi stands to suffer to some extent from a reduction of exports to South Africa.

Botswana will suffer rather little from the pass-through effects of sanctions on South Africa. Diamonds are a strong source of export earnings and government revenues and there are possibilities of exporting meat by air. She may benefit from diversion of air traffic if Zimbabwe suspends air links.

While the potential losses from sanctions and related actions appear to be smaller for Zambia than for Zimbabwe, nevertheless Zambia is in such a fragile economic condition that any losses will be hard to bear. Zambia has suffered from the prolonged depression of the price of copper, her staple export, and has been in economic decline over most of the past decade. There is a backlog of investment in the mines. The mining industry now provides only about 15 per cent of government revenue. Some progress was made in bringing the balance of the budget under control between 1982 and 1983, but the deficit has ballooned again since then and may have amounted to a third of GDP in 1986. The annualized rate of growth of broad money increased from 17 per cent at the end of 1984 to over 40 per cent (estimated) by the end of 1985. The external deficit on current account widened from 10 per cent of GDP in 1984 to 17.2 per cent in 1985. Arrears on external debt-service payments have reached alarming proportions and the availability of loans from foreign banks has decreased.[1]

Zambia faces a major task in developing other forms of economic activity to offset the reduced contribution of copper and in escaping from her overwhelming problem of external debt. With the help of good rains and a policy of increasing prices to farmers, Zambia has had considerable success in the recent past in increasing her degree of self-sufficiency in food.[2] This achievement, however, could be endangered by a combination of urban resistance to higher food prices and budgetary stringency. Towards the end of 1986, in order to reactivate a standby credit from the IMF, the Government of Zambia doubled the price of maize in order to reduce the subsidy burden on the budget. This led to serious rioting in the copper towns and the Government felt obliged to restore the subsidy. The Government wishes to avoid reducing prices to farmers and is looking for budgetary savings to offset the cost of the restored food subsidies.

In short, Zambia is a country in deep economic trouble, without further exacerbation of her situation from the outside.

Up to the present, the economic problems of Zimbabwe are by no means as acute as those of Zambia. The balance on current account has been kept under control, but at the expense of stringent rationing of foreign exchange. Shortage of currency for the purchase of imported capital goods and inputs is a serious handicap to economic activity and the capital stock has become progressively more antiquated. Unemployment is high. The budget deficit has increased to 12-13 per cent of GDP and an IMF programme for the country collapsed in March 1984. The defence of the Beira corridor — Zimbabwe's railway, road and pipeline link with the sea — is a heavy burden. External debt-service liabilities, including liabilities to the IMF, are reported to amount to over 30 per cent of export earnings. Only limited relief could be secured by blocking financial transfers to South Africa and this could well be outweighed by South African retaliation. In these conditions, any loss of foreign-exchange earnings would aggravate problems, which are already severe; and depression of demand in South Africa could seriously affect the viability of various manufacturing activities.

COSTS TO NEIGHBOURING COUNTRIES OF IMPOSING SANCTIONS

As has been seen in Chapter 2, the Prime Minister of Zimbabwe has threatened to apply the Commonwealth package of sanctions against South Africa, with certain additions. The President of Zambia has advocated sanctions, but has been less specific about the action he might take. At the end of 1986, Prime Minister Mugabe and President Samora Machel, of Mozambique, met and renewed their call for mandatory sanctions; but a few days later Mr Mugabe said that the necessary preliminary studies were still not complete. This may well indicate an increasing appreciation of the costs and risks. As to Botswana, Swaziland and Lesotho, it seems likely that their governments will fall back on the escape clause in the Commonwealth agreement, arguing that to impose sanctions would be excessively damaging to them.

If the Government of Zimbabwe were to carry out its stated intention of imposing the Commonwealth package of measures with the stated additions, then — leaving aside for the moment the risks of South African retaliation — the measures with the greatest significance for the Zimbabwean economy would be the suspension of air links, prohibition of purchases from South Africa of iron, steel and coal (or, in this instance, coke), abrogation of the trade agreement and suspension of financial transfers to South Africa.

It is difficult to form a clear view of the effects of suspending air links. At present, the roughly 38 flights per week between Harare and Bulawayo and various points in South Africa are the most profitable (or least unprofitable) part of Air Zimbabwe's operations. It is possible though that, if these flights were discontinued, there would be an almost equivalent gain in traffic *via* intermediate points such as Gabarone. It is also possible that Air Zimbabwe may gain from the suspension of direct flights between Australia and South Africa.

Over recent years, Air Zimbabwe has been making increasing losses. The subsidy bill to the already over-burdened Zimbabwe budget is put at Z$12 million in 1985/86 and Z$45 million for 1986/87.[3] Efforts are said to be in hand to reduce these losses. Zimbabwe Airways could be severely hit if, by way of retaliation, South Africa were to withdraw servicing facilities.

Suspension of direct air links could also have indirect effects. For example, some firms operating in Zimbabwe fear that maintenance engineers might be reluctant to come to Zimbabwe if they had to fly by an indirect route. At the least, the cost of commercial contacts would increase.

There is a two-way trade in steel products between Zimbabwe and South Africa, with some degree of specialization on both sides. In 1984, Zimbabwe imported from South Africa steel products worth Z$27.3 million.[4] No doubt there would be possibilities of replacing these imports either by domestic production or by imports from other sources, through Beira if other routes were closed off, but at considerable extra cost.

Zimbabwe would suffer difficulties both in the short and in the longer term if she were to consider that the Commonwealth package necessitated an embargo on imports of South African coke. Zimbabwe is highly dependent on low-sulphur coke from South Africa for production of ferro-chrome for export. Alternative supplies would be unduly costly (quite apart from possible transport problems). At present, also, the Wankie furnaces are closed for renovation, so that in the short term Zimbabwe is also dependent on South African coke for steel production.

A ban on government procurement in South Africa might have only comparatively minor effects. But there could be substantial problems if it were extended to companies in Zimbabwe (notably in the construction and building, chemical and pharmaceutical sectors) which supply the Zimbabwean Government and buy inputs from South Africa.

A ban on government contracts with majority-owned South African companies would raise difficult questions of which suppliers should be disqualified, since the majority ownership of most major companies operating in Zimbabwe is at any rate nominally outside South Africa.

Major losses could arise from abrogation of the bilateral trade agreement, renewed in 1976, which gives preferential access to Zimbabwean goods in the South African market. Zimbabwean exports to South Africa of manufactures, worth some Z$80 million in 1985, would be particularly at risk — the more so if the Zimbabwean Government were to suspend trade assistance, including the 9 per cent tax-free export incentive, for goods destined for South Africa. Given high transport costs, Zimbabwe would have difficulty in finding alternative export markets for these goods, at any rate without substantial terms-of-trade losses.

On the other side of the account, Zimbabwe could save foreign exchange by suspending transfers to South Africa. For 1985/86, pension payments to residents of South Africa are estimated at Z$63 million and dividend payments at Z$25 million. South African transfers to Zimbabwe in 1984 are put at Z$23 million — Z$15 million of dividends, profits *et cetera*, Z$7 million of payments for services and Z$1 million of pension payments.[5] Thus Zimbabwe would gain as long as South Africa limited herself to retaliating in kind.

Given all the imponderables, it is very difficult to assess what would be the cost to Zimbabwe (or to Zambia, or to the other neighbouring countries) of imposing sanctions on South Africa, supposing that the South African authorities did not choose to retaliate. Such an assessment might in any case be beside the point, given the substantial risks of retaliation, which might well be considerably more damaging to the neighbouring countries than the costs they would incur directly by imposing sanctions.

Vulnerability over Transport

Outweighing all other points by far is the dependence of the neighbouring countries on transport for their exports and imports by way of South Africa — transport links which can be cut if the South African Government chooses to retaliate against or put pressure on neighbouring countries.

There are five important ports joined to the neighbouring countries by rail and road links without passing through South Africa (see the map).

To the west, a railway runs from Zambia, through southern Zaire and Angola, to Benguela (Lobito). The theoretical capacity of the line and of the port of Lobito is put at 2.3 million tonnes a year (total of traffic in both directions).[6] By mid-1975, however, this railway was coming under heavy pressure by the Unita rebels in Angola (who receive material support not only from South Africa but also from the United States). This line has now been unusable for Zambia and Zaire for many years and the prospects for its re-opening in the near future are not favourable. Much of the traffic from and to the mineral-rich south of Zaire now passes through the long railway route by way of Zambia, Zimbabwe and South Africa.

To the north-east, Zambia is connected to Dar es Salaam in Tanzania, 2,000 km away, by the Tazara railway, a road and a pipeline. The utility of the railway has been affected by the breakdown of locomotives, disruption of sections of track by floods, pilferage and poor telecommunications with Dar es Salaam. The capacity of the port of Dar es Salaam is limited and it has to handle much of Tanzania's external trade as well as the traffic from and to Zambia. In 1984, the railway line had to be closed for four months. Capacity was improved by the arrival of fourteen West German locomotives in 1983, but in no year has the line been able to handle more than about 1.2 million tonnes of freight, less than half the designed capacity.[7] Work is in progress, supported by foreign aid, to improve these routes.

The most natural route to the sea from Zimbabwe is by railway, road and pipline east through Mozambique to the port of Beira. These routes are subject to continuing harassment by the Renamo guerillas in Mozambique, commonly held to be supported by the South African security

FIGURE 4.1

The Railways and Ports of Southern Africa

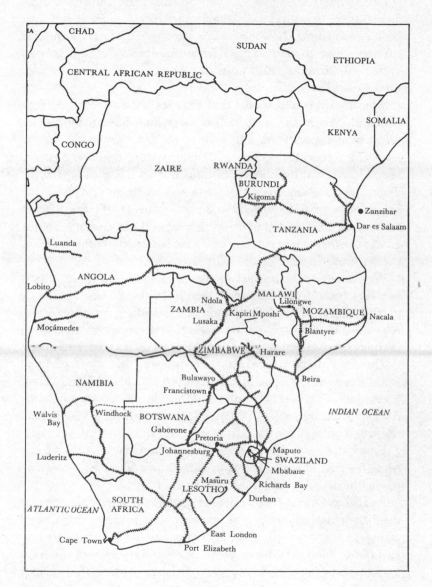

forces, but efforts are being made to rehabilitate the railway and port and to defend them from attack (see below).

There is also a railway line wholly through Zimbabwe and Mozambique to the port of Maputo (the Limpopo line). Here again, there is an aid-supported effort to rehabilitate the line. Its eastward end, however, runs through sparsely populated country close to the South African border so that it is very vulnerable to attack and no traffic has gone over this line for three years.

The natural access to the sea for Malawi is through Mozambique to the port of Nacala (which has an estimated, theoretical capacity of 1.8 million tonnes per year). In the highly unsettled conditions in Mozambique, this line has also been closed, but it is hoped to reopen it in the spring of 1987. There is a railway, too, from Malawi to Beira and there are possibilities of transport by road to connect with the Tazara railway to Dar es Salaam — although these depend on the goodwill of the Government of Zambia as well as the carrying capacity of this northern route.

Botswana has the advantage that three-quarters of her export earnings come from diamonds, which can be flown out directly to the north. These diamonds are handled by the (South African-controlled) Central Selling Organization; but it is, perhaps, unlikely that this would take action to jeopardize Botswana's diamond earnings. Increasing amounts of meat from Botswana are being air-freighted to the Middle East. Botswana is very much more vulnerable on the import side. A very high proportion of her imports, including cereals and energy, comes from South Africa.

Finally, Lesotho is entirely surrounded by South Africa, while Swaziland's sole access to the sea, avoiding South Africa, is *via* the highly vulnerable route to Maputo.

Available figures for the degree of dependence of the various neighbouring countries on exports to, imports from and transport by way of, South Africa show a fair degree of variation. This may be in part because they refer to different periods, with differing degrees of disruption of the various transport routes. Also, while some of the figures apparently include exports to and imports from South Africa herself, others may not. Subject to these reservations, however, the following figures may give a general impression of the dependence of neighbouring countries on transport by way of South Africa.

TABLE 4.1

Percentage of External Trade of Neighbouring Countries Passing *via* South Africa

	Exports			Imports		
	Leistner	*Wilsenach*	*Silavecky*	*Leistner*	*Wilsenach*	*Silavecky*
Zimbabwe	65	65-90	92	68	65-80	93
Malawi	50	50	60	60	60	n.a.
Zambia	40	40	39	70	70	67
Zaire	[45]	n.a.	n.a.	57	n.a.	n.a.

SOURCES: G.M.E. Leistner, 'Sanctions against South Africa in Regional Perspective', *Africa Institute of South Africa Bulletin*, Vol. 25, No. 5, 1985; the estimates are said to have been made in October 1983 and are attributed to G.G. Maasdorp, *Transport Policies and Economic Development in Southern Africa* (Durban: Economic Research Unit, University of Natal, 1984). The actual figures given for exports from Zaire are 45 per cent of copper, 60 per cent of lead and zinc, 40 per cent of cobalt.

Andre Wilsenach in the *Africa Institute of South Africa Bulletin*, cited in *The Star*, Johannesburg, 20 November 1986.

Zdenek Silavecky, *An Assessment of the Likely Effects of S.A. Economic Sanctions Upon: A. Countries of the Region; B. Zimbabwe*, mimeograph (Harare: Standard Chartered Bank Zimbabwe Ltd., 1986). Figures for rail traffic only.

In the six months April-September 1986, South African Railways carried roughly 1.6 million tonnes of exports from, and 2.3 million tonnes of imports into, neighbouring countries (annual rates, not seasonally adjusted). Some 1.3 million tonnes of exports from neighbouring countries went out through South African ports and 0.6 million tonnes of imports came in.

While there is thus a fair amount of information on rail traffic in Southern Africa, G.M.E. Leistner, the Director of the Africa Institute of South Africa, has commented that:

TABLE 4.2

Freight from and to Neighbouring Countries Handled by
South African Railways and Ports
(April-September 1986, annual rate not seasonally adjusted)
(thousand tonnes)

	Exports		*Imports*	
	via *South African Railways*	*Through South African ports*	via *South African Railways*	*Through South African ports*
Zimbabwe	789.8	556.6	1,191.6	359.4
Malawi	37.0	36.8	110.4	25.0
Zambia	107.0	102.4	69.4	3.4
Zaire	215.0	214.8	153.2	15.0
Botswana	16.2	0.4	379.8	51.8
Swaziland[a]	399.8	350.0	48.0	6.4
Lesotho[b]	9.4	3.6	378.2	104.4
Total	1,574.2	1,264.6	2,330.6	565.4

SOURCE: South African Transport Services.

[a]In addition Swaziland exported over 27,600 tonnes and imported over 62,200 tonnes by South African Transport Services road services in the period April 1986 to January 1987.

[b]In addition, Lesotho exported over 1,700 tonnes and imported over 678,500 tonnes by South African Transport Services road services in the period April 1986 to January 1987.

'Virtually nothing is being published on intra-regional goods traffic by road and air...

'It is known, though, that a few large road carrier undertakings based in South Africa play a crucial role in conveying urgently needed spares, machinery, pharmaceuticals, consumer goods *et cetera* from South African ports and factories to customers throughout the region. This vital traffic is supplemented by Safair's fleet of freight planes flying between Jan Smuts Airport and destinations all over Africa.'[8]

Given that there is some scope for switching freight from one route to another, the problems which could arise in the event of prolonged interruption of routes by way of South Africa may be best illustrated by some very approximate figures relating to the neighbouring countries as a group. The total traffic of these countries to and from the outside world appears to be of the order of 7 million tonnes a year (total of traffic in both directions excluding traffic to and from Angola, Mozambique, Swaziland and Lesotho). Of this, the Tazara railway might be able to carry something of the order of 1.5 million tonnes. The Beira route is currently carrying 1 million tonnes a year or slightly more, although of this 600,000 tonnes is imports into Zimbabwe of petroleum and petroleum products through the pipeline. (Some specialized and volatile petroleum products are imported into Zimbabwe from South Africa.) Recently press reports that about 60 per cent of the external freight traffic of the neighbouring countries currently goes to, from or through South Africa may be about right.[9]

A major effort at rehabilitation is being put into the port of Beira and the rail and road links with Mozambique. This work is being financed in part, but by no means wholly, by aid from the outside world. It is hoped that, by the end of 1989, the Beira corridor might be able to carry 5 million tonnes per year (total of traffic in both directions, including the flow through the pipeline). This compares with some 4.7 million tonnes actually carried on this route in 1963/64.

Achievement of the target cannot be taken for granted, given the amount of work to be done and, too, the risks of sabotage and armed interference. In relation to all the routes through Mozambique, it seems highly unlikely that the state of civil war or anarchy will end in the foreseeable future: it is doubtful whether the Renamo guerrillas, even if they were to prevail, could form an effective government and Frelimo, forming the present government, could well prove an even more disruptive opposition. Moreover, many observers believe that, in conditions of increased friction between South Africa and Zimbabwe, the South African security forces could and would carry out or organize increased disruption. The Government of Zambia is said to fear sabotage of bridges on the Tazara railway by forces based in Malawi.

Re-establishment of more direct transport routes to the sea would not only remove the main risks of transport disruption by South Africa. It would also reduce costs of transport (notably for Zimbabwe and Malawi) in spite of the subsidies by which the South African authorities try to perpetuate the dependence of the neighbouring countries on the routes to the south. For Zimbabwe, annual payments for freight through South Africa amount to Z$225 million of which, it is said, Z$85 million could be saved by increased use of the shorter Beira route. Against this potential saving, however, Zimbabwe is meeting part of the costs of rehabilitation and it is commonly conjectured that the defence of the transport routes by Zimbabwean troops costs something of the order of Z$1 million a day, half or more of budgeted defence spending, roughly 10 per cent of central government expenditure, or 3 to 4 per cent of GNP. In other words, this cost would amount to almost half of the budget deficit, which is giving rise to considerable anxiety. (But the figure is a rough, hearsay estimate and it is not clear whether it purports to refer to the additional cost involved by the operation, or the total cost including pay and equipment for troops who would be maintained in any case.) In addition to the costs of the operation, it is said that news of casualties, which is beginning to trickle out, could become a political liability to the Government.

Much will depend on the rate at which the carrying capacity of the routes to the east and north can be increased. Zambia may be able to carry on at any rate the bulk of her external trade *via* Dar es Salaam, although further work is needed to reduce costly delays. On the other hand, Zimbabwe (and, of course, Lesotho and Swaziland) will remain highly vulnerable to disruptions of traffic *via* South Africa.

If transport routes through South Africa were blocked on a prolonged basis, Zimbabwe would face very serious loss of foreign-exchange earnings and difficult choices of priorities for exports through the Beira corridor. Priority might be given to tobacco because of its high value per tonne and labour-intensity in production (between 85,000 and 100,000 people employed). This would be at the expense of exports of minerals (other than gold, which can be air-freighted). Sugar growers could turn to crops for consumption locally or in neighbouring countries, but these might be less labour-intensive, an important consideration when there is large and growing unemployment.

If access to the sea through South Africa were suspended or curtailed for a prolonged period, the authorities in Zimbabwe would be reluctant to allow competition from neighbouring countries for the limited carrying capacity of the Beira corridor. There have already been warnings that Zimbabwe might have to suspend transit facilities for Zaire, which would have to attempt to export minerals from the south of the country through the Voie Nationale to the north, coping as well as possible with the additional costs and capacity constraints involved. Malawi is already unable to export sugar because of high transport costs; and, because her Government is considered too friendly to South Africa, she risks losing her outlets through neighbouring countries — the more so if these neighbours are limited in their access to the sea.

OTHER ASPECTS OF VULNERABILITY

The emphasis so far has been on the effects on the export earnings of South Africa's neighbouring countries of a possible prolonged blockage of transport through (and to) South Africa, since this shows in the most clear and dramatic form the extreme vulnerability of these countries to determined retaliatory action if the South African Government were to decide to take this course. But there are many other ways in which the neighbouring countries could be harmed by South African actions, even of a selective nature.

Zimbabwe can meet a major part of her requirements for petroleum products through the Beira pipeline (so long as this and the port installations are not sabotaged). Zambia has her own refinery, importing oil through a pipeline from Dar es Salaam. Other countries of the region are highly dependent on imports of petroleum products from South Africa. Lesotho, Swaziland and parts of Mozambique, Zimbabwe and Botswana receive power from the South African Electricity Supply Commission.

Dependence on food imports varies from country to country and from year to year. Zimbabwe and Malawi are self-sufficient or more than self-sufficient in staple foods in good years, but are vulnerable to failures of the rains. Botswana, on the other hand, is highly dependent on imports of grain. With the help of good rains, Zambia has had considerable success in the recent past in increasing her degree of self-sufficiency in food. This achievement though could be jeopardized if the combination of the political strength of the towns and budgetary stringency were to lead to a reduction of prices paid to farmers.

Zimbabwe's dependence on South Africa for coke and various steel products has been noted above. Some chemicals used as inputs in production processes have a short shelf-life and, if not imported from South Africa, would have to be brought in by air, with the attendant costs. Otherwise some export earnings would be jeopardized (if not already hit by transport problems in exporting).

More generally, it is sometimes suggested that the neighbouring countries suffer from the fact that trade is largely in the hands of the subsidiaries of South African firms or of people who automatically look to South Africa as the source of supply and that they would benefit from shopping around more broadly for imports. There are no doubt cases of goods which could be obtained more cheaply elsewhere than from South Africa, provided that transport facilities permit; but there are other cases in which government policies of procurement outside South Africa have involved considerable additional costs.

As already mentioned, Zimbabwe's export earnings would be hit if the South African Government were to abrogate the bilateral trade agreement.

Another form of retaliatory action open to the South African Government is the expulsion of migrant workers. In October 1986, after a land mine explosion near the border which injured six soldiers, the South African Government decreed that Mozambican workers in South Africa would be repatriated after completion of their contracts and that no more would be recruited. There have been reports that this ruling has subsequently been relaxed, but the threat of similar action in the future remains.

Botswana, Lesotho and Swaziland are bound to South Africa by the operation of the Southern African Customs Union (SACU). Under the SACU arrangements, all customs duties on imports into Lesotho, Swaziland and Botswana as well as South Africa herself are collected by the Republic (which determines the rates of duty). Lesotho, Swaziland and Botswana receive payments out of the pool of duties collected. These are calculated on the countries' shares in total imports from the outside world two years previously, with an addition of 42 per cent as a rough compensation for inflation in the interim and for the effects of protective tariffs on the prices of goods bought from South Africa. About 70 per cent of Lesotho's government revenues, 65 per cent of those of Swaziland and some 20 per cent of those of Botswana come from the SACU pool. The South African Government normally wishes to appear scrupulous in honouring its contractual obligations and it appears highly unlikely that it would withold SACU payments from the three countries — or, indeed, that these three countries will follow policies which might provoke such retaliation.

The three countries might possibly benefit from winding up the arrangement and operating their own individual tariffs and collecting their own customs revenue, but this would involve considerable administrative costs.

COUNTER-MEASURES BY NEIGHBOURING COUNTRIES

Since it is clear that retaliatory action by South Africa could have devastating effects on at least some of the neighbouring countries, it is natural to ask whether these countries have weapons at their disposal to deter the Government of South Africa from taking really damaging action.

One evident threat would be the expropriation of South African investments in the neighbouring countries. Given that dividend payments are already limited by the tax systems and exchange controls in force in these countries, expropriation would do them little good (and would risk the loss of experienced managers and other personnel); and, by the same token, the threat of expropriation might well be ineffective as a deterrent to the South African Goverment. Zimbabwe did in fact suspend dividend payments in 1984, but has permitted them again from the beginning of 1986. The effect of taxation, including a 20 per cent tax on permitted dividends, is such that South African investors can only repatriate about 19 per cent of profits earned. (This, obviously, provides a strong incentive to reinvest profits in Zimbabwe.) Net remittances of dividends *et cetera* from Zimbabwe to South Africa have been estimated at about US$7 million per year, or only about 0.04 per cent of South Africa's total foreign-exchange earnings.[10]

The Prime Minister of Zimbabwe has threatened to suspend remittances to South Africa of pensions of former Rhodesian civil servants. These are estimated at US$40 million a year — 0.2 per cent of South Africa's current foreign-exchange receipts — going to about 40,000 people, or about 1.5 per cent of the white South African electorate.[11] Again, the threat is not a persuasive one.

In general, it is clear that the balance of power is strongly on the side of South Africa.

PROSPECTS FOR RETALIATION BY SOUTH AFRICA

The preceding section has considered the vulnerability of the neighbouring countries if the South African Government were to choose to retaliate in fairly extreme form against sanction actions by them. It is now necessary to consider what forms any reaction by the Government of South Africa would in fact be likely to take.

The authorities in Pretoria have been at pains to distinguish between action in response to security threats — notably incursions and sabotage by ANC guerillas — and measures in response to economic action. Security threats are held to justify military action; economic sanctions might be met by economic counter-measures.

Some measures, which would be highly damaging to neighbouring countries, would have relatively negligible costs in relation to the size of the South African economy. For example, carriage of goods for neighbouring countries contributes only about 3 per cent of the revenue of South African Transport Services — R300 million, or three-quarters of one per cent of South African's exports of goods and services as in 1985.[12] Some commentators make much of the value of South Africa's exports to and trade surplus with the neighbouring countries; but, in the three years 1983-85 only about 4 per cent of South Africa's merchandise exports went to destinations in the whole of Africa and perhaps 3 per cent to Zimbabwe, Zambia, Zaire and Malawi, the neighbouring markets most likely to be cut off by sanction measures.

There has been concern in Pretoria though to present measures affecting the neighbouring countries as being in accordance with the norms of international law. This may tend to inhibit action which could be represented as disproportionate to any sanctions which may be imposed by neighbouring countries. Many measures disruptive to neighbour countries, however, can be and have been represented as taken for domestic reasons — diversion of rolling stock to other parts of the railway system, tightening up of border formalities and so on.[13]

Companies in South Africa with interests in neighbouring countries naturally apply such pressure as they can to the Government to refrain from action which would damage their economic interests, but they are by no means confident that their views will prevail.

The most likely reaction to sanctions by neighbouring countries, it is widely considered, is a continuation of cat-and-mouse actions, together with tailored and more-or-less proportionate responses to particular sanctions. There is a long and well-documented history of South African cat-and-mouse actions against neighbouring countries, both military and economic.[14] Many of these actions appear to have been designed to warn neighbouring countries of their vulnerability, or to discourage them from taking hostile actions. Immediately after the 1986 Commonwealth meeting to discuss sanctions against South Africa, the South African authorities imposed a 25 per cent surcharge against imports consigned to Zambia, to be rebated when the goods were in fact shown to have been imported by Zambia. This measure was justified as protection against the sale in the South African market of goods nominally addressed to Zambia and on which South African duty and tax had not been paid. At the same time, South Africa increased the rigour of her customs checks on the Zimbabwean border, causing substantial delays. These measures were rescinded in a matter of weeks. The timing of their imposition may or may not have been coincidental. Similar measures have been taken on various other occasions.

If the Government of Zimbabwe were to carry out its threat to suspend air links with South Africa, the South African authorities might, perhaps, consider themselves justified in cutting back the carriage of Zimbabwean goods by rail. If Zimbabwe were to prohibit imports of South African coal, the South African authorities might ban exports to Zimbabwe of coke needed for metallurgical processes. If Zimbabwe were to suspend imports of South African steel, the Government of South Africa would presumably prohibit imports of steel from Zimbabwe. And so on.

These are examples of possible limited and proportional responses. But if South Africa were assailed by really severe sanctions from the outside world and from her neighbouring countries, the Government might conceivably consider that it was in a state of all-out conflict and that more severe measures against the neighbouring countries were justified. On the other hand, as already mentioned, there are business interests in South Africa with a stake in the economic viability of the neighbouring countries and, moreover, the Government in Pretoria must have, at worst, ambivalent feelings about political instability on its borders. Nevertheless, if the governments of Zimbabwe and Zambia were to institute fairly extensive sanctions against South Africa while the other neighbouring countries did not, the South African Government might possibly wish to show a sharp contrast in its treatment of its actively hostile and its more compliant neighbours.

What will in fact happen cannot be predicted with any degree of confidence. Probably the most likely outcome is a continuation of cat-and-mouse, together with related and proportional responses to particular actions taken by neighbour countries. It may well be that the neighbouring countries, having reflected on the costs to themselves of sanction actions and the risks of highly damaging retaliation, may decide to do nothing, or at least to keep their threats in abeyance. The prospect then would be for a continuation of cat-and-mouse action by South Africa. It is necessary to recognize though that such a prognostication could be overtaken by events even before this essay is published.

AID TO THE NEIGHBOURING COUNTRIES

Advocates of severe sanctions against South Africa tend to assume that the adverse effects on the neighbouring countries should and would be alleviated by increased aid from the outside world.

The question arises not only whether aid is likely to be forthcoming in sufficient amounts but also how far and how fast it could alleviate the problems.

The neighbouring countries are already receiving aid, notably to improve the transport route *via* Beira. As has been seen, though, it will take at least two years to complete the present phase of the work and even then carrying capacity will be limited in relation to the expected volume of traffic. Progress is affected by the security situation along the route.

Professor Reginald Green, of the Institute of Development Studies at the University of Sussex, in the United Kingdom, has estimated that, in the event of severe disruption, the neighbouring countries might well require initial support of $US750-1,000 million, plus US$250-500 million per year thereafter.[15] These sums are largely but not wholly additional to existing aid flows — roughly US$1.2 billion to the neighbouring countries in both 1984 and 1985.[16] Joseph Hanlon, in a study for the Catholic Institute of International Relations in London, suggests that Professor Green's figures may be a little on the low side.[17] Donor countries — notably the United Kingdom and United States — made substantial new commitments of aid at the beginning of 1987; but it is not clear that these will lift disbursements above the level of 1984-85.

In the worst eventuality, severe disruption of transport routes, the affected countries would need not only to be compensated for their losses of export earnings but also to receive help in obtaining imports essential to economic activity and human welfare, if necessary by a sort of 'Berlin air-lift'. No doubt rehabilitation and expansion of capacity of the routes *via* Maputo, Beira, Nacala and Dar es Salaam could be further speeded up if sufficient resources were made available (although a strong command structure would also be necessary). For the Maputo, Beira and Nacala routes, the problem would remain of protecting the reconstruction work, and transport along the routes, from disruption by Renamo, possibly strongly supported by South Africa. Representatives of the United States and the United Kingdom and others are reported to have warned the governments of the neighbouring countries against imposing sanctions on South Africa.[18] It is by no means clear that donor governments would be prepared to compensate the neighbouring countries for additional costs arising from their own actions. Some of the neighbouring countries might hope to receive aid from the Soviet Union; but informed observers have the impression that the Soviet Union is following a policy of reducing its involvement in the area.

NOTES AND REFERENCES

1. *Financial Times*, London and Frankfurt, 15 December 1986.

2. *Financial Times*, 22 October 1986.

3. Zdenek Silavecky, *An Assessment of the Likely Effects of SA Economic Sanctions Upon: A. Countries of the Region; B. Zimbabwe*, mimeograph (Harare: Standard Chartered Bank Zimbabwe, 1986).

4. *Ibid*.

5. *Ibid*.

6. The capacity figures used in this section are attributed to the Secretariat of the Southern African Development Coordination Conference (SADCC). SADCC was set up after the accession to independence of Zimbabwe in 1980, by the 'Front Line States' (Angola, Botswana, Mozambique, Zambia, Zimbabwe and Tanzania), together with Malawi, Swaziland and Lesotho, '...to liberate our economies from their dependence on the Republic of South Africa, to overcome the imposed economic fragmentation and to co-ordinate our efforts toward regional and national economic development'.

7. *The Star*, Johannesburg, 20 November 1986.

8. G.M.E. Leistner, 'Sanctions against South Africa in Regional Perspective', *Africa Institute of South Africa Bulletin*, Vol. 25, No. 5, 1985.

9. See, for example, *The Times*, 7 February 1987. Alternative estimates of 85 per cent (for example, *The Times*, 11 February 1987) appear too high, even if Swaziland and Lesotho are included.

10. Estimates by Mr Silavecky.

11. Estimates by Mr Silavecky.

12. Figures given orally to the present writer by the Director-General of South African Transport Services.

13. See, for example, Joseph Hanlon, *Beggar Your Neighbours* (London: Catholic Institute for International Relations, 1986).

14. Hanlon, *op. cit.*

15. The analysis has been published as Reginald Green, 'Sanctions and SACC Economies', *Third World Review* (London: Third World Foundation, 1987).

16. Net disbursements of official development assistance; from *Development Cooperation, 1986* (Paris: Organisation for Economic Cooperation and Development, 1987).

17. Hanlon, *op. cit.*

18. *The Times*, 24 February 1986.

Chapter 5

Costs to Countries Imposing Sanctions

THE POSSIBLE costs to neighbouring countries if they take various types of economic action against South Africa have been considered in the course of Chapter 4. It remains to consider costs incurred by countries outside Southern Africa as a consequence of sanctions imposed by themselves or by others (including costs of possible retaliatory actions by South Africa). This chapter focusses, in particular, on costs to the United Kingdom.

TYPES OF COST

The possible costs to countries outside Southern Africa are of several kinds:

(a) costs arising from loss of export earnings as a results of (i) reduction of South Africa's capacity to import and (ii) retaliatory action by South Africa;

(b) costs which might arise from the loss of supplies from South Africa of certain minerals;

(c) loss of other imports from South Africa or possible additional costs of replacing them from other sources;

(d) reduction of dividend receipts (i) from South Africa and the neighbouring countries as a result of decreased profitability of operations there and (ii) from South Africa as a result of controls imposed by the authorities;

(e) suspension of debt-service payments by South Africa and/or by neighbouring countries; and

(f) costs arising from suspension of air services.

LOSS OF EXPORT EARNINGS

South African imports of goods and non-factor services were already depressed in 1985 and the first three quarters of 1986, when they were just over 3 per cent less than in 1978-79 (at 1980 prices) and 21 per cent less than in 1980-82. This depressed level of imports of goods and services was, of course, associated with depressed levels of domestic spending; but South Africa would in any case have needed to run a large surplus on current account in 1985 to accommodate to capital outflows without excessive loss of reserves.

For the future, it has been suggested in Chapter 3 that South Africa may need to maintain surpluses on current account of the order of R5-6 billion per year, as at 1985 prices, if she is to continue to repay external debt 'at a reasonable rate' in the absence of net new capital inflows. On top of this, sanctions — according to their degree of severity — could reduce merchandise export earnings by anything between, say, 5 and 25 per cent. This would be equivalent to reductions of imports of goods and non-factor services, as in 1985, of between 6 and nearly 32 per cent. (Of South Africa's imports of goods and non-factor services in 1985, roughly 80 per cent were goods [f.o.b. values] and 20 per cent services.)

In 1985, the United Kingdom exported goods to South Africa to the value of £1 billion (down from £1.2 billion in 1984), or some 1.3 per cent of total merchandise exports (down from 1.7 per cent in the previous year). If the United Kingdom were to lose visible exports *pro rata* with the reduction of South Africa's capacity to import goods and non-factor services, then the loss of exports (assuming no compensatory gains elsewhere) would be of the order of £50-250 million per year, or 0.06-0.32 per cent of total merchandise exports.

There are no published figures for the United Kingdom's exports of services to particular countries. It seems reasonable to assume that South Africa derives most of her imports of non-factor services from the major industrial countries. Taking account of the comparative advantage of the United Kingdom in the export of services, its share in South Africa's imports of non-factor services might be about a quarter.[1] South Africa's imports of non-factor services in 1985 were of the order of R5 billion, or about £1.7 billion. Thus British exports of services to South Africa in 1985 may have been of the order of £0.4 billion.

Various estimates have been made of the loss of jobs which might result from sanctions. In answer to a question in the House of Commons (24 June 1986), the British Minister for Trade, Alan Clark, stated that, 'given the current levels of trade with South Africa, our best estimate is that the equivalent of 120,000 United Kingdom jobs may be involved in the export of goods and services to that country'. The same figure has been used by the Prime Minister and the Foreign Secretary and may be regarded as the officially approved estimate. If the jobs 'involved' were reckoned *pro rata* with the reduction of South African imports by between 5 and 25 per cent, the number would be scaled down to between 6,000 and 30,000. On the one hand, though, these figures do not take account of the 21 per cent decrease in the volume of South Africa's imports of goods and non-factor services which had already occurred in 1985 (by comparison with 1980-82). On the other hand, they do not take account of compensatory mechanisms — a possible marginal effect on the sterling exchange rate leading to increased export sales elsewhere and stimulus to production for the home market, increased efforts to sell in other markets, possible effects in limiting wage claims in affected industries and the influence of higher unemployment on government policies.

While exports to South Africa are a rather small proportion of total British exports, South Africa is a more important market for particular items. For example, 2.1 per cent of exports of chemicals (SITC 5) and 1.9 per cent of exports of machinery and transport equipment (SITC 7) went to South Africa in 1985 (2.5 per cent and 2.8 per cent respectively in 1984); and the proportions would be considerably higher for individual items. Thus reductions of exports to South Africa resulting from sanctions could increase difficulties in particular sectors or, in other terms, could make some small addition to the overall task of adjustment and restructuring.

The greater importance of South Africa as a market for some products than for others gives rise to fears of South African retaliation — for example, a ban on imports of Scotch whisky. While the South African Government may be more inclined to strike back at smaller economic powers than at the United States, the British Government has been a voice for moderation in the international sanctions debate and it is not clear that the South African Government would see any advantage in singling out the United Kingdom for retaliation.

In estimating the potential cost of losses of exports to South Africa, it is necessary to bear in mind that the alternative to imposing sanctions on South Africa, and bearing the costs, may be loss of trade with other African and Third World countries.

SUPPLIES OF STRATEGIC MINERALS

It has been suggested in Chapter 2 that governments of industrial countries are unlikely to deny themselves supplies of strategic minerals from South Africa; and that the South African Government is unlikely to withhold such supplies by way of retaliation or warning against sanctions, since it will not wish to lose the export earnings or to encourage the development of alternative supplies or of substitutes.

Nevertheless, the fear of shortages of certain minerals, or of excessive dependence on supplies from countries of the Eastern trading area (the Soviet Union and countries of Eastern Europe) has been an element in thinking about policy towards South Africa.

For several at least of these minerals (for example, chrome, manganese, vanadium and the platinum group) alternative sources are being developed. The United States has stockpiles of various minerals, including enough chromium for 26 months, manganese for 39 months and platinum for ten months.

Moreover, experience shows that, in conditions of short

supply and consequent high prices, substitution tends to be much greater than might have been expected in advance. For example, the United States Mineral Advisory Board has estimated that over 30 per cent of current consumption of chromium could be replaced immediately by available substitutes and that in five to ten years some two-thirds of total consumption could be replaced by the substitutes currently recognized.

TABLE 5.1

Strategic Minerals: Shares in World Exports, 1983
(per cent)

Commodity	*South Africa*	*CMEA countries*
Manganese metal	80	3
Vanadium	49	12
Chrome ore	27	40
Ferrochromium	54	7
Platinum group	28	33
Alumino-silicates	52	—
Manganese ore	30	17
Ferromanganese	23	1
Antimony trioxide	40	15

SOURCE: Minerals Bureau of South Africa.

DIVIDEND RECEIPTS

Payments to foreigners of dividends, branch profits and other such investment income in 1985 amounted to R1.27 billion (US$0.57 billion), down from an average of R1.39 billion (US$1.38 billion) in 1981-83. (Of these, only branch profits, around 2 per cent of the total in recent years, include sums accruing to foreigners but reinvested in South Africa.)

For the United Kingdom, the Foreign and Commonwealth Office has said the following:

'According to the most recent triennial survey of UK direct investment overseas, the book value of UK direct investment in South Africa at the end of 1981 was £2,826 million (including banking, insurance and oil). ...a very rough estimate of the book value of UK direct investment, based on the annual flows of investment and taking account of exchange-rate fluctuations, indicate[s] that it was worth approximately £3 billion at end-1984 and approximately £2 billion at end-1985. Unofficial estimates put the value of UK portfolio investment in South Africa at £6 billion. These figures must, however, be treated with considerable caution. In present circumstances the realizable value seems likely to be much lower for direct and portfolio investment alike. The sterling value of earnings from these assets is also limited by the fall of the Rand and the imposition of South African exchange controls.'[2]

Sanctions and related developments could also limit receipts of dividends from the neighbouring countries. As has been seen, however, these are limited already by high rates of tax and exchange controls.

DEBT SERVICE

When South Africa entered into debt negotiations in November 1984, her foreign debt was valued at US$23.7 billion. Of this, some US$14 billion was included in the arrangements for deferral of amortization, although interest payments on the whole debt have continued. Interest payments to foreigners in 1984 were of the order of US$1.8 billion. Since the latter part of 1984, there has been considerable net repayment of debt in spite of the 'standstill' arrangement.

While it appears that the South African authorities would be very reluctant to suspend debt-service payments, it seems by no means impossible that severe curtailment of the capacity to import as a result of sanctions could lead them to declare *force majeure*.

Sanctions-related developments could increase the debt-servicing difficulties of other countries of Southern Africa. (The situation of Zambia, in particular, already gives rise to anxiety.) External debt at the end of 1984 was: Zambia, US$3.5 billion; Zimbabwe, US$2.23 billion; Malawi, US$0.83 billion; and Botswana, Swaziland and Lesotho combined, US$1.05 billion.[3] Zambia's contractual debt-service payments in 1987, on debt already outstanding at the end of 1984, were put at US$124 million interest and US$280 million amortization, those of Zimbabwe at US$113 million interest and US$208 million amortization.[4]

While the debt and debt-service liabilities of Southern African countries are small in relation to those of major debtor countries such as Brazil, Mexico and Poland, nevertheless suspensions of debt-service payments or outright repudiation of external debt would still be highly unwelcome to creditor banks, central banks and governments of creditor countries in the present situation of widespread debt problems.

SUSPENSION OF AIR SERVICES

It has been seen that British Airways and other airlines flying to South Africa, together with their governments, would be very reluctant to suspend services and suffer the attendant diminution of profits.

Problems might arise from the denial of over-flying rights by African countries, forcing airlines, if they continued services, to use longer and more costly routes.

Among non-neighbour African countries, Kenya in particular would suffer from suspension or re-routing of air services to South Africa. It is estimated that at present landing fees for flights to and from South Africa, and other benefits such as improved air-freight services to Western Europe, benefit Kenya to the tune of $50 million per year.[5]

NOTES AND REFERENCES

1. This assumed share of a quarter is equal to the United Kingdom's share in recent years in South African merchandise imports from the United Kingdom, the United States, West Germany and France.

2. Memorandum by the Foreign and Commonwealth Office, reproduced in *South Africa*, Sixth Report of the Select Committee on Foreign Affairs, House of Commons, *op. cit.*, Vol. I, Appendix A, p. xxxiv.

3. *World Debt Tables, 1985-86* (Washington: World Bank, 1986).

4. *Ibid*.

5. *Financial Times*, 18 December 1986.

Chapter 6

Summary and Conclusions

THIS ESSAY considers the economic effects which sanctions and related actions against the Republic of South Africa may have on the country itself, on the neighbouring countries and on the rest of the world. It takes account of possible repercussions such as retaliatory actions by South Africa against neighbouring countries.

EXTENT OF SANCTIONS AGAINST
SOUTH AFRICA

Economic sanctions and related actions against South Africa began to have serious effects in 1985 and 1986. Beginning in July 1985, a number of major banks in the United States and elsewhere refused to roll over their loans to South Africa. In September 1986, the European Community agreed on a prohibition of imports of South African iron and steel and in the following month the United States Congress overrode the President's veto and imposed the broadest package of sanctions yet adopted by any major economic power. The Prime Minister of Zimbabwe and the President of Zambia have threatened to implement a package of sanctions agreed in the Commonwealth (with some additions in the case of Zimbabwe); but the threats had not been implemented up to mid-February 1987. It appears unlikely that the other neighbouring countries will attempt to take economic measures against South Africa.

The greatest impact so far comes from a virtual cessation

of capital inflows as a result of declining confidence in the future of the South African economy and pressures on firms and banks to sever their connections with the Republic. If South Africa is to continue to repay external debt at a reasonable rate, it is considered that she will have to continue to run surpluses on current account of the order of R5-6 billion a year (as at 1985 prices), thus cutting into the capacity to import and the supply of resources available for investment and other internal purposes.

Trade sanctions imposed up to February 1987 are fairly limited in their impact on the South African economy as a whole, the most important being the widespread prohibition of imports of South African iron and steel. But sanctions may well escalate if governments and public opinion in the rest of the world remain dissatisfied with political developments in South Africa. If there were considerable further escalation of trade sanctions, the essay suggests that they might possibly reduce merchandise export earnings by almost a quarter. To maintain the required surplus on current account would then require a reduction in imports of goods and non-factor services by some 30 per cent in real terms, by comparison with 1985. This, very rough, estimate of the possible loss of export earnings is based on the common assumption that no effective action could or will be taken to reduce South African earnings from gold, diamonds and strategic minerals. Given this assumption, many observers would consider a loss of export earnings of 20 per cent or more to be very much an extreme case, given the possibilities of circumventing sanctions.

EFFECTS OF SANCTIONS ON
SOUTH AFRICA

There are widely differing views on the economic effects on the Republic of South Africa of sanctions, boycotts and divestment by foreign companies. Some South Africans look for a boost to the economy, at any rate in the short term, through increased stimulus to import substitution, possibly encouraged by quantitative restrictions on imports. Others point to the probable high cost of increased import substitution and hope that sanctions and related measures may strengthen the arguments, on both economic and social grounds, for policies designed to promote more labour-intensive development.

Rough estimates, set out in the Appendix, suggest that, with a continuation of the present economic structure, near-cessation of capital inflows coupled with continued repayment of debt may lead to something like stagnation of GDP (and hence to a decline of per capita GDP). Increased trade sanctions might then lead to an actual decrease of GDP. With net capital outflows, investment in import-substitution projects would be at the expense of other forms of productive investment; and lack of business confidence may be a continued drag on the economy. The conclusion of a paper from the South African Federated Chamber of Industries (on its intermediate sanctions scenario) of a fall in GDP of some 17 per cent and of employment by about 14 per cent over five years, may be too severe, but it cannot be wholly discounted. Sanctions and divestment will tend to increase South Africa's technological lag.

Much will clearly depend on the future course of sanctions and related actions; and on government policies and other reactions in South Africa. The response to more severe sanctions might well be import controls and an increase in the already excessive government regulations, leading to still greater economic inefficiency.

There is a strong case for policies making for much more labour-intensive development, but these are not easy to devise and implement. (Further relaxation of regulations on small businesses would make a useful contribution.) Even with a marked shift in policy, unemployment is likely to continue to increase, among whites as well as among other races, and the more so if sanctions escalate further. The result can only be a further increase of turbulence in the black townships, leading to a continuation and even an increase in repressive measures. A marked decrease of GDP could reduce the resources available to the Government of South Africa, but it seems natural to suppose that other programmes, including those of benefit to non-whites, would be cut before expenditures on the police and armed forces. Increased unemployment and fear of unemployment among whites may lead some to press for reform, but will strengthen others in their support for repressive policies.

There could be a vicious spiral in which dissatisfaction with political developments in South Africa leads to further escalation of sanctions; and these, in turn, strengthen the forces inimical to political and social reform. Some advocates of sanctions no doubt look to a revolutionary outcome, with all the political, social and economic risks which that would involve.

EFFECTS ON NEIGHBOURING COUNTRIES

Any depression of economic activity in South Africa reacts to the disadvantage of the neighbouring countries, through a decrease in South African demand for goods and services and a possible reduction in employment of migrant workers. But the costs to neighbouring countries will be increased if they themselves impose sanctions on South Africa and the costs could be very much greater still if South Africa steps up her actions against them in retaliation.

Remittances from migrant workers in South Africa are said to contribute as much as half of GNP in Lesotho, 6 per cent in Swaziland, 3 per cent in Mozambique, 2 per cent in Malawi and 1 per cent in Botswana. If Zimbabwe were to share *pro rata* in a 30 per cent decrease in South Africa's imports, this would reduce her merchandise export earnings by, say, 3-5 per cent. Some manufacturing activities would be seriously affected and the loss of export earnings, while not catastrophic, would further exacerbate the already serious shortage of foreign exchange. Botswana and Zambia would be less affected; but Zambia is already in a very serious balance-of-payments crisis without any further aggravation.

Against the costs, there may be gains for neighbouring

countries which are prepared to play host to activities designed to circumvent sanctions on South Africa.

If some neighbouring countries impose sanctions on South Africa, they could gain by suspending interest and dividend payments and financial transfers to South Africa, provided that this gain was not wiped out by retaliatory measures. If the Government of Zimbabwe were to prohibit imports of steel or coke from South Africa, the costs of replacement from alternative sources would be high and economic activity, including production for export, would suffer. Suspension of air links could increase the losses of Air Zimbabwe, which have contributed to the country's budgetary problems, while Botswana might gain from diversion of traffic.

The greatest threat to neighbouring countries lies in the possibility of retaliatory action by the Government of South Africa. The countries most likely to be affected are Zimbabwe and Zambia, which have threatened to impose economic measures against South Africa. At present, 60 per cent of the external trade of the neighbouring countries is said to go to, from or *via* South Africa. Efforts are being made, with the help of foreign aid, to reduce dependence on transport by way of South Africa; but continuing civil war in Mozambique hampers the rehabilitation of direct transport routes to the Indian Ocean and transport vulnerability will remain acute at least for some considerable time to come. Zimbabwe's export earnings would be further reduced if South Africa were to abrogate the bilateral trade agreement. The South African authorities could inflict economic damage by cutting supplies of goods and services which could only be obtained elswhere at a much higher cost, particularly while the transport problem remains. It is not clear to what extent neighbouring countries could count on aid donors to compensate them for such losses.

It is by no means certain that the Government of South Africa will go beyond the sort of cat-and-mouse tactics it has employed *vis-à-vis* the neighbouring countries up to the present; but, the greater the pressure put on South Africa by her neighbouring countries and by the rest of the world, the greater may be the temptation in South Africa to demonstrate the vulnerability of the more hostile of her neighbours.

Costs to Other Countries of Imposing Sanctions

Sanctions reduce South Africa's capacity to import from the rest of the world and might lead to retaliation against particular exports from sanctions-imposing countries. Official estimates that the equivalent of 120,000 jobs in the United Kingdom may be involved in the export of goods and services to South Africa cannot be taken to imply that anything like this number of jobs is in fact at risk as a result of sanctions; but the effects of sanctions make an unwelcome, if relatively small, addition to the general task of economic adjustment and restructuring.

It seems unlikely that industrial countries will deliberately deny themselves supplies of strategic minerals from South Africa; or that South Africa will deliberately withhold supplies of these minerals (although some suggest that South Africa might attempt to boost her export earnings by limiting supplies).

A greater risk to outside countries is of reduction of investment earnings or loss or further postponement of debt-service payments, both from South Africa and from neighbouring countries. South Africa has already negotiated a postponement of amortization of a considerable part of her external debt. The South African authorities are reluctant to suspend interest payments, but might be seriously tempted or feel obliged to declare *force majeure* if sanctions led to a further considerable reduction of the capacity to import. Of the neighbouring countries, Zambia and Zimbabwe carry heavy burdens of external debt and could be pushed into default if their economic difficulties increase further. South Africa's external debt is in excess of US$20 billion. Zambia's external debt at the end of 1984 was US$3.5 billion, Zimbabwe's US$2.23 billion and Malawi's US$0.83 billion. The figures are considerably smaller than those of such major debtor countries as Brazil, Mexico and Poland; but any aggravation of the existing, widespread debt service problems would be unwelcome.

Appendix

South Africa: Adjustment in the Face of Sanctions

THE ESTIMATES of the potential effects of sanctions on the South African economy, made in the Federated Chamber of Industries, plausibly assume that South Africa would not have the option of external borrowing to make good any loss of export earnings (or increase in the cost of imports) resulting from trade sanctions: indeed, that South Africa would need to maintain surpluses on current account of R5-6 billion (as in 1985) to repay external debt 'at a reasonable rate'. With a given target for the balance on current account, any decrease in export earnings would have to be offset by an equal decrease in imports. As has been seen, the paper assumes that this would be brought about by some combination of reduction of government expenditure, increase of interest rates, depreciation of the exchange rate and direct import controls.[1]

The intermediate case in the Federated Chamber's paper suggests that the 'inter-industry effect' of trade sanctions would be a fall of GDP by 6.7 per cent. While the meaning of the inter-industry effect is not entirely clear, this may correspond with the estimate in Chapter 3 that severe trade sanctions might lead to a loss of export earnings equivalent to 7 per cent of GDP. The Federated Chamber's paper then estimates that the 'total net effect' over five years would be a decrease in GNP of 16.9 per cent — 2.5 times as great as the inter-industry effect. How plausible is this estimate? On what assumptions does it depend?

A SIMPLE MODEL

It has not been possible to find out how the adjustments to trade sanctions and their effects are simulated in the model used. To check the plausibility of the estimates, it has therefore been necessary to go back to square one, devising a model which appears reasonable, but which may or may not be closely similar to the model used for the Federated Chamber's paper.

The model used in this paper has three stages.

The first stage estimates the effects on GDP, over five years, of different rates of capital inflows or outflows, all other things remaining unchanged.

The second and third stages estimate the effects of trade sanctions of varying degrees of severity (assuming throughout a continuing capital outflow of R6 billion per year, as simulated in stage one).

Other things including external capital flows remaining unchanged, a given loss of export earnings resulting from sanctions would necessitate an equal reduction of imports of goods and services. Stage two considers the adjustments necessary to adapt to a decreased capacity to import and the possible effects on GDP.

The third stage then looks at the dynamic effects, over five years, of any reduction of GDP postulated by the first stage: reduction of GDP would be likely to lead to diminution of savings, hence of investment and hence of productive capacity and the growth of GDP.

The estimates are in terms of 1985 prices throughout.

DIFFERENT ASSUMPTIONS ON NET
EXTERNAL CAPITAL FLOWS

In the first stage, growth of GDP is assumed to depend on an increase of the stock of fixed capital. Gross capital formation is financed by national savings (that is to say, total savings generated in the economy, minus net interest, dividends and other factor income payments to foreigners), plus net capital inflows. If there is net capital outflow (necessitating an excess of exports of goods and non-factor services over imports similarly defined) this is an additional charge on domestic savings. (In South African usage — for example, in the statistics published by the Reserve Bank — the term 'domestic savings' is used for savings after subtraction of net interest, dividends and other factor income accruing to foreigners. In what follows, by analogy with the established usage for national and domestic product, the term 'domestic savings' will be used to denote gross savings generated in South Africa, before deduction of net interest, dividends and other factor income payable to foreigners.)

According to the national accounting figures published by the Reserve Bank, gross domestic savings, as just defined, varied between 25.9 and 30.6 per cent of GDP over the four years 1982-85. In the four previous years, the gross domestic savings rate had varied between 32.4 per cent and 37.3 per cent. Although increases of government current expenditure tend to cut into domestic savings, it seems reasonably conservative to assume, for the purpose of this stage of the projections, a gross domestic savings rate of 27 per cent of GDP throughout.

The Reserve Bank publishes figures for the size of the fixed capital stock and for depreciation. While such figures are inescapably problematical, they are taken here as implying:

(a) that the ratio of fixed capital stock to GDP has progressively increased over the years to around 3:1; and

(b) that depreciation in each year has been of the order of 5.5 per cent of the capital stock in the previous year (which, of course, includes assets with a relatively long life, such as roads, railways, mine workings and buildings, as well as things with shorter lives, such as machinery, equipment and vehicles).

In the projections, it will therefore be assumed that maintenance of productive capacity requires investment in each year equal to 5.5 per cent of the capital stock in the previous year (that is, about 16.5 per cent of GDP).

Investment in stocks (change in inventories) has swung

violently from positive to negative in recent years, in rhythm
with increases and decreases of GDP. Disinvestment in stocks
over the four years 1982 to 1985 was equal at 1980 prices
to rather more than 7 per cent of GDP as in 1985, and there
was a further reduction in the first two quarters of 1986,
approximately offset by an increase in the the third quarter.
It appears, therefore, that an upturn in economic activity
would depend on fairly considerable investment in stocks. In
the projections, it is assumed that an increase of stocks would
amount to 75 per cent of increases of GDP. This might appear
a fairly drastic assumption. (The logic of the projections is
that greater use of savings for an increase of stocks means less
increase in the fixed capital stock and so in productive
capacity.) The assumption, however, is consistent with
experience over the three years of economic growth,
1979-81.[2] In any case, an alternative assumption of
investment in stocks at a flat rate of 1 per cent of GDP —
which seems low against the background of the large running-
down of stocks in 1982-85 — leads to only minor changes in
the results shown in Table A.1 below.

Then, given gross national savings as they emerge from the
estimates, assumed net capital inflows or outflows and the
estimates for depreciation and investment in stocks, net fixed
investment is derived as a residual. The capital stock increases
by the amount of net investment in each year (or decreases
if gross fixed investment is insufficient to cover depreciation),
and the change in the capital stock affects the requirement
for depreciation in the following year.

Next, GDP is assumed to change in each year by an amount
equal to one-third of net investment (or disinvestment) in fixed
capital (that is to say, the net incremental capital-output ratio
is assumed to be equal to the estimated average capital-output
ratio of about 3:1).

In arriving at gross national savings from gross domestic
savings, it is necessary to subtract net interest, dividends and
other factor income accruing to foreigners. On a crude
extrapolation from past experience, net interest and other

investment income accruing to foreigners is put at 10.5 per cent of net external liabilities as in the previous year. Net external liabilities are increased or reduced each year by the assumed amount of net capital inflow or outflow. No revaluation of net external liabilities, as at 1985 prices, has been assumed. Factor income other than interest, dividends and other investment-related payments is assumed to continue at R2 billion per year — possibly an exaggeration if there were a large-scale reduction of the foreign labour force.

Base figures for 1986 (at 1985 prices) were then derived from the national accounting figures for the first three quarters of

TABLE A.1

Projections for the South African Economy Showing the Effect of Differing Capital Inflows or Outflows

Assumed annual net flow of external capital (R billion)	*GDP in 1992 (1987 = 100)*	*Average rate of growth of GDP, 1987-92 (per cent per annum)*
+ 6	112.8	2.4
0	107.2	1.4
− 6	101.5	0.3

SOURCE: Author's projections.

1986 and by applying the assumptions of the model to the latest available figures for the capital stock and for net external liabilities.

The model is then used to estimate the effects on the rate of growth of GDP over five years of different assumed levels of net capital inflows or outflows from 1987 onwards. (Here and elsewhere, any change of reserves is considered to be included in the assumed net flow of external capital.) As a basis of comparison for the further estimates set out below, projected GDP in 1987 is put at 100. (In considering the relatively small spread of growth rates between the three cases, it is necessary to bear in mind that greater net capital inflows is taken to entail greater net investment income liabilities to foreigners and greater growth of GNP to necessitate larger investment in stocks.)

RELATIONSHIP BETWEEN REDUCTIONS
IN IMPORTS AND IN GDP

Given the assumed need to maintain surpluses on current account of R6 billion a year, a reduction of export earnings as a result of trade sanctions can be taken as necessitating an equal reduction in the value of imports of goods and services. Merchandise exports are larger in value than imports of goods and non-factor services (that is to say, excluding payments of interest, dividends and other factor income), so that the maximum assumed reduction of export earnings, of the order of 23 per cent, would necessitate a reduction of imports of goods and non-factor services by almost 30 per cent.

Imports may be reduced by direct import controls, increased rates of import duty, or depreciation of the exchange rate (which would also provide a stimulus to exports, so far as sanctions may allow). However, a decrease of imports reduces the resources available for domestic use (and increase of exports may depend on diversion of resources from production for domestic use). Consequently, the adjustments required to maintain a given surplus on current account in the face of a substantial loss of export earnings would be likely to involve contractionary monetary or fiscal measures to avoid excessive inflationary pressure. The Reserve Bank figures show 23 per cent under-utilization of manufacturing capacity in June 1980; but such a figure is inescapably problematical and, at the same time, the rate of inflation (consumer prices) was not far short of 18 per cent.

In recent years there have been several cases of large increases or decreases in imports of goods and non-factor services, accompanying corresponding increases or decreases in total use of resources (both in constant, 1980 prices; total use of resources is defined as private consumption plus government consumption, plus gross investment plus exports). In each case, the percentage change in imports was considerably greater than that in total use of resources in the same year. (Between 1978 and 1979, imports of goods and services decreased by 1.4 per cent while total use of resources increased by 2.3 per cent, while between 1985 and the first

TABLE A.2

South Africa: Relationship between Use of Resources and Imports of Goods and Non-factor Services

	Percentage changes		Absolute changes (R million at 1980 prices)		
Years	Total use of resources	Imports of goods and non-factor services	Total use of resources (A)	Imports of goods and non-factor services (B)	(A) as multiple of (B)
Increases					
1979-80	+ 8.4	+ 19.6	+ 6,090	+ 2,780	2.2
1980-81	+ 6.6	+ 13.1	+ 5,187	+ 2,229	2.3
1983-84	+ 7.7	+ 20.0	+ 5,855	+ 2,681	2.2
Decreases					
1981-82	− 4.2	− 15.6	− 3,512	− 2,999	1.2
1982-83	− 5.4	− 17.1	− 4,361	− 2,767	1.6
1984-85	− 3.7	− 14.4	− 3,059	− 2,317	1.3

SOURCE: Derived from South Africa Reserve Bank, Pretoria, *Quarterly Bulletin*, December 1986.

three quarters of 1986, both increased, but by only small percentages.) When the changes are compared in absolute, constant rand terms, it will be seen from the table that in each case the change in total use of resources was considerably greater than that in imports. The differences ([A] as a multiple of [B]) were greater in the periods when both use of resources and imports increased than when both declined. On a more sophisticated analysis, a distinction could be made between the fluctuations and a declining trend in the ratio of imports of goods and services to total use of resources.

For the present purposes, it may be noted that, between 1981 and 1985, there were three year-to-year declines of imports of goods and services, in real terms, of between 14.4 and 17.1 per cent. Reductions of imports of goods and services of this order of magnitude were compatible with reductions in total use of resources between 1.2 and 1.6 times as great in absolute terms in the same period.

How great would have to be the contraction in total use of resources, at any rate in the short term, to allow a 30 per cent reduction of imports? Imports of goods and non-factor services did in fact decrease by 30 per cent (at 1980 prices) between 1981 and 1983, the absolute decrease in total use of resources being some 1.4 times as great. This decline in imports, however, was from a high base, 34 per cent above the average as in 1978-79, while imports of goods and non-factor services in 1985 and the first three quarters of 1986 were a little less than the average for 1978-79. Thus if the reduction of the capacity to import as a result of trade sanctions were anything like as much as 30 per cent from the base level of 1985, and if this were to occur over a fairly short period of time, it could be said to be outside the range of recent experience.

In Table A.3, Case I is nevertheless based on the assumption that it would be possible to bring about a decrease of imports of goods and non-factor services of the order of 30 per cent with a decrease in total use of resources only 1½ times as great in absolute terms. The first row in the table shows the base figures for exports, imports and use of resources on the basis of GDP = 100 (based on the national accounting figures for 1985 at current prices). The table then investigates the possibly extreme case envisaged in the main text — apparently rather similar to the intermediate scenario in the Federated Chamber's paper — of a reduction of merchandise export earnings by roughly 23 per cent, equal to 7 per cent of base GDP. In order to maintain the required balance on current account, imports of goods and non-factor services would also need to be reduced by an amount equal to 7 per cent of base GDP. If this required a reduction in total use of resources one-and-a-half times as great, the reduction in the use of resources would be 10.5 per cent of GDP.

. TABLE A.3

South Africa: Short-term Effects of Loss of Export Earnings
(all 'absolute' figures are scaled to base GDP = 100)

| | Exports | | Use of resources | | Imports of goods and non-factor | |
	Goods	Non-factor services	Domestic	Total	services	GDP
Base figures (absolute)	30.1	3.7	89.9	123.7	23.7	100.0
Case I Absolute changes	− 7.0	—	− 3.5	− 10.5	− 7.0	− 3.5
Percentage changes	− 23.3	—	− 3.9	− 8.5	− 29.5	− 3.5
Case II Absolute changes	− 3.5	—	− 10.5	− 14.0	− 7.0	− 7.0
Percentage changes	− 11.6	—	11.7	11.3	− 29.5	− 7.0

SOURCE: *Quarterly Bulletin*, South African Reserve Bank, Pretoria, December 1986; author's estimates.

If the reduction of export earnings were all on the side of volume, so that use of resources to produce exports decreased by 7 per cent of base GDP, then the implied, residual reduction of use of resources for domestic purposes (consumption plus investment) would be 3.5 per cent of base GDP, or 3.9 per cent of domestic use of resources as at the base level. GDP would decline by 3.5 per cent (decrease in use of resources less decrease in imports). Thus in the fairly short term a 23 per cent reduction of exports would lead to a 3.5 per cent contraction of GDP and a 3.9 per cent contraction in domestic use of resources.

This result, though, assumes that a contraction of export earnings would lead to an equal release of resources for alternative, domestic uses. Against this, part of the reduction of export earnings resulting from sanctions may be assumed to result from price discounts. This would not release resources required for the production of exports. Moreover, reductions in the volume of exports would not necessarily make available resources which could readily be put to work to produce goods and services for the home market.[3] Case II is based on two assumptions which might be regarded as at the opposite extreme from Case I:

(a) that half the loss of export earnings results from price discounts; and

(b) that none of the resources released by the contraction in the volume of exports can be put to alternative uses.

The whole of the reduction in the use of resources of 10.5 per cent of base GDP, needed to maintain the required balance on current account, would then have to be borne by production for the domestic market. The contraction of total use of resources, including the contraction amounting to 3.5 per cent of base GDP in the resources used in producing exports, would amount to 14 per cent of base GDP. GDP (domestic use of resources plus exports minus imports) would decrease by 7 per cent and domestic use of resources by 11.7 per cent.

This 7 per cent decrease of GDP may be compared with the conclusion in the Federated Chamber's paper that the total net effect over five years, on the intermediate scenario, would be a decrease in GDP of some 17 per cent. On the reasoning in this Appendix, the discrepancy could be accounted for by two elements:

(a) that the reduction in the use of resources would have to be considerably more than one-and-a-half times the required reduction in imports; and

(b) that the resulting reduction in GDP would lead to a reduction of savings, so that it would not be possible to maintain the productive capacity of the capital stock.

ESTIMATES INCLUDING DYNAMIC
EFFECTS

Initial adjustments as illustrated in Table A.3 would be likely to lead to decreases in savings in two ways:

(a) even if there were no depression of the ratio of gross domestic savings to GDP, a reduction of GDP would lead to a reduction of the absolute amount of savings; and

(b) a reduction of incomes would be likely to depress the overall savings rate.

The projection model underlying Table A.1 was used to investigate the degree of depression of the aggregate savings rate which would be required to lead to a decrease of GDP by some 17 per cent over five years.

If the initial downward adjustment in GDP were 7 per cent, as in Case II in Table A.3, then the depression of the savings rate necessary to produce the stated result would be from 27 per cent in the base case to 22 per cent. The further assumption has been made of no further disinvestment in stocks (running down of inventories) in spite of the decline in GDP.

For illustrative purposes, if it were assumed that there would be no depression of the gross domestic savings rate below 27 per cent then, in order to arrive at a decrease of GDP by 17 per cent after five years, it would be necessary that the initial decline of GDP in adjustment to the decrease of export earnings should be of the order of 12.5 per cent. But this might appear somewhat artificial, since an initial depression of GDP of this order might well lead to a gross domestic savings rate well below 27 per cent.

COMMENTS ON THE FEDERATED CHAMBER'S
ESTIMATES

The estimates in this Appendix depend on a number of assumptions which are open to challenge. They may, however, provide a framework against which to judge the plausibility of the estimates in the Federated Chamber's paper.

On a straightforward interpretation of the 'inter-industry effect' shown in the paper, the scenario showing the largest effect on the economy would appear extreme, given the assumption of no measures adversely affecting earnings from gold and strategic minerals. The intermediate case may perhaps be taken as representing the strongest impact to be expected from even severe trade sanctions.

On the intermediate scenario, the 'total net effect' after 5 years is estimated as a decrease of GDP by some 17 per cent, two-and-a-half times as great as the initial 'inter-industry effect'. On the reasoning in this Appendix (to recapitulate), the considerably greater depressive effect on GDP after five years must come from some combination of

    (a) the depression of GDP needed to sustain the required balance on current account in the face of loss of export earnings (that is to say, to reduce absorption of imports),

    (b) a decrease of savings arising out of this depression of GDP and

    (c) a depression of the ratio of gross domestic savings to GDP as a consequence of lower incomes.

The paper claims to have taken account of import substitution allowed by the present under-utilization of capacity. Nevertheless, it may assume a contraction in the use of resources — to adjust to the reduction in capacity to import — rather greater than that suggested by experience in recent years.

It may also assume a fairly considerable depression in the overall savings rate in response to depression of incomes. Judgment on this element would depend on refined econometric work, beyond the scope of this essay.

The paper assumes no new investment for import substitution. Many commentators lay considerable stress on the scope for import substitution. It has to be remembered, however, that import substitution, beyond the fuller utilization of existing capacity, is likely to depend on investment and that, with continuing net capital outflows, capacity to invest will be limited. Indeed, it has been pointed out in the literature that all production catering to domestic demand is import substitution in the sense that it absorbs purchasing power which could otherwise be spent on imports. The only way of breaking out of the constraint imposed by the limited supply of savings available for the finance of investment is by increasing the labour-intensity of production (thus somewhat moderating the unemployment problem).

In conclusion, it is only possible to say that the estimate of a decrease in GDP over five years of 17 per cent, as a result of trade sanctions, may be excessive but cannot be dismissed with any degree of certainty.

NOTES

1. Some commentaries have been in terms of the 'export multiplier' — the proposition that loss of export income will lead to reductions of expenditure, thus reducing incomes and expenditures elsewhere in the economy, so that the final income loss will be some multiple of the original loss in the export sectors. Such an approach, however, is inappropriate in judging the effects of sanctions over the medium term, given the possibilities of macro-economic adjustment available to the authorities. The paper from the Federated Chamber correctly focusses on the adjustments necessary to sustain the required balance on current account in the face of net capital outflows and a loss of export earnings.

2. A regression for the period 1979-85 (in 1980 prices) gives the result:
annual change in inventories = 0.85 x change of GDP - R822 million
(R^2 = 0.703)

3. In two of the cases of reduction in use of resources shown in Table A.2, the reduction of export volume accounted for only a small part of the total. In 1982-83, exports accounted for 26 per cent of the reduction in total use of resources. It may not be coincidental that this year shows the highest ratio of reduction in use of resources to reduction in imports.

List of References

THIS list contains only the more important references cited in the text. The reader should refer to the Notes and References at the end of each chapter for more complete bibliographical information.

M.S. DAOUDI AND M.S. DAJANI, *Economic Sanctions: Ideals and Experience* (London: Routledge & Kegan Paul, 1983).

BRIAN DOLLERY, *Has the Divestment Issue been Carefully Considered?* (Johannesburg: South African Institute of International Affairs, 1986).

The Effect of Sanctions on Employment and Production in South Africa: a Quantitative Analysis, mimeograph (Pretoria: Federated Chamber of Commerce, 1986).

GROUP OF EMINENT PERSONS, *Mission to South Africa: the Commonwealth Report* (Harmondsworth, Middlesex: Penguin, 1986).

JOSEPH HANLON, *Beggar Your Neighbours* (London: Catholic Institute of International Relations, 1986).

GARY CLYDE HUFBAUER and JEFFREY J. SCHOTT, *Economic Sanctions in Support of Foreign Policy Goals*, Policy Analyses in International Economics No. 6 (Washington: Institute for International Economics, 1983).

CAROLYN M. JENKINS, *The Economic Implications of Disinvestment for South Africa* (Johannesburg: South African Institute of International Affairs, 1986).

G.M.E. LEISTNER, 'Sanctions against South Africa in Regional Perspective', *Africa Institute of South Africa Bulletin*, Pretoria, Vol. 25, No. 5, 1985.

G.M.E. LEISTNER, 'Economic Interdependence in Southern Africa', *Africa Institute of South Africa Bulletin*, Pretoria, Vo. 26, No. 4, 1986.

DAVID LEYTON-BROWN (ed.), *The Utility of International Economic Sanctions* (London and Sydney: Croom Helm, 1987).

MERLE LIPTON, *Capitalism and Apartheid: South Africa 1910-1984* (Aldershot, Brookfield and Sydney: Gower, 1985).

P.A. NEL, *An Assessment of the Development and Welfare of Employees in the Republic of South Africa*, Research Report No. 133 (Pretoria: Bureau of Market Research, University of South Africa, 1986).

ROBIN RENWICK, *Economic Sanctions*, Harvard Studies in International Affairs No. 45 (Cambridge, Massachusetts: Institute of International Studies, 1981).

ANTHONY SAMPSON, *Black and Gold: Tycoons, Revolutionaries and Apartheid* (London, Sydney, Auckland and Toronto: Hodder & Soughton, 1987).

ZDENEK SILAVECKY, *An Assessment of the Likely Effects of SA Economic Sanctions upon: A. Countries of the Region; B. Zimbabwe*, mimeograph (Harare: Standard Chartered Bank Zimbabwe, 1986).

South Africa: Minutes of Evidence and Appendices, Sixth Report of the Select Committee on Foreign Affairs, House of Commons, Session 1985-86 (London: Her Majesty's Stationery Office, 1986).

List of Thames Essays

OCCASIONAL papers of the Trade Policy Research Centre are published under the omnibus heading of Thames Essays. Set out below are the particulars of those published to date. The first 44 titles were published under the Centre's sole imprint, but they may also be obtained from the Gower Publishing Company, its address in the United Kingdom, the United States of America and Australia being set out in the reverse of the title page of this essay.